1866-1991

125th

ANNIVERSARY

RUSSIAWALKS

This is the
Henry Holt Walks Series, which originated with
PARISWALKS *by Alison and Sonia Landes.*
Other titles in this series include:

LONDONWALKS *by Anton Powell*
JERUSALEMWALKS *by Nitza Rosovsky*
FLORENCEWALKS *by Anne Holler*
ROMEWALKS *by Anya M. Shetterly*
VIENNAWALKS *by J. Sydney Jones*
VENICEWALKS *by Chas Carner and Alessandro Giannatasio*
BARCELONAWALKS *by George Semler*
NEW YORKWALKS *by The 92nd Street Y*

RUSSIAWALKS

David and
Valeria Matlock

An Owl Book

Henry Holt and Company • New York

Published by Henry Holt and Company, Inc.,
115 West 18th Street, New York, New York 10011.
Published in Canada by Fitzhenry & Whiteside Limited,
195 Allstate Parkway, Markham, Ontario L3R 4T8

Library of Congress Cataloging-in-Publication Data
Matlock, David.
Russiawalks / David and Valeria Matlock.—1st ed.
        p.   cm.
"An Owl book."
Includes index.
1. Moscow (R.S.F.S.R.)—Description—Tours   2. Leningrad
(R.S.F.S.R.)—Description—Tours. I. Matlock, Valeria. II. Title.
III. Title: Russiawalks.
DK597.M38 1991
914.7'31204854—dc20   91-3152
                                                          CIP
ISBN 0-8050-1204-4 (alk. paper)

Henry Holt books are available at special discounts
for bulk purchases for sales promotions, premiums,
fund-raising, or educational use. Special editions
or book excerpts can also be created to specification.
For details contact:
Special Sales Director, Henry Holt and Company, Inc.,
115 West 18th Street, New York, New York 10011

First Edition—1991

Designed by Claire Naylon Vaccaro
Maps by Jeffrey L. Ward
Printed in the United States of America
Recognizing the importance of preserving the written word,
Henry Holt and Company, Inc., by policy, prints all of its
first editions on acid-free paper. ∞
1   3   5   7   9   10   8   6   4   2

Facing title page: *View from inside the Belltower of Ivan the Great*

FOR OUR PARENTS

Jack and Rebecca Matlock
Nina Arkadeva
Konstantin Strukov

Contents

Acknowledgments

Many people have helped bring this book to light of day. Our agent, Ivy Fischer Stone, deserves special thanks for support well beyond the call of duty. Theresa Burns, always tactful and patient, has been as perfect an editor as any writer could wish. And our original editor, Peter Bejger, talking with Ivy, proposed the idea of our doing *Russiawalks* in the first place. Fifi Oscard, as always, has continued to be a source of reassurance and support.

Special thanks are due to the staffs of many museums in Moscow and Leningrad: at the Kremlin, where, on very short notice, we were given access to areas closed to the public; at the Museum of the History of the City of Moscow, whose research library we made free use of; at the Winter Palace and Hermitage; and at the many church and literary museums scattered throughout the two cities.

We must also thank Edward Kasinec and the whole staff of the Slavonic Division of the New York Public Library, where we have done so much of our research.

John Blee has been a friend throughout the writing, and any aesthetic sensibility in succeeding pages is probably due to his influence, or to long telephone conversations with Vadim Strukov, our brother and brother-in-law, who has provided both inspiration and advice. And we thank our parents, to whom this book is dedicated, for putting us up for long months in both Moscow and Leningrad.

RUSSIAWALKS

Introduction

What would these strangers? Know their minds, Boyet.
If they do speak our language, 'tis our will
That some plain man recount their purposes.
Know what they would.
                    —*Rosaline, in* Love's Labor's Lost

Ever since Muscovy rose up as if out of nowhere into Elizabethan awareness, Russians have been an exotic people. Shakespeare's playful tone soon evaporated as ambassadors and merchants recounted the horrors of Ivan the Terrible's reign. "Yt was God that suffereth this wicked people, whoe live, flow and wallowe, in the verie hight of their lust and wickedness of the crienge Sodomiticall sines, to be thus justly punished and plaged with the tirrainie of so bloudye a kynge," wrote Sir Jerom Horsey after his sojourn in the distant land.

Memoirists never tired of reciting alleged Russian propensities for sin and cruelty, charges that went unrebutted because the number of English-speaking Russians was so tiny. Two and a half centuries later, the 1839 memoirs of the French Marquis de Custine in such vein were bitterly denounced by Russian intellectuals, who were by then far more familiar with foreign tongues. Outsiders who drew close to the czar's court provided vivid witness of public executions and grand drunken banquets. Many were shrewd observers of the pathology of absolute autocracy. But they were less sensitive to more attractive strains in the society that found expression in worship, guarded conversation, and secret clubs.

Perhaps it was the language barrier, or the caution of a population wary of the secret police, but foreigners had a difficult time discerning dissidence, which runs as deeply in the society as autocracy. Few are so naive today. Nevertheless, Churchill's famous description of Russia as "a riddle, wrapped in a mystery, inside an enigma" seems as true now as it did fifty years ago—sometimes, one would think, even for Russians.

Our aim is not to eliminate Russia's aura of mystery, which is half the fun of being there. But we do propose to bring you into the aura, face to face with both the "enigma" and the "riddle." Our means are unorthodox: walking and looking. There may be better ways of getting to know a country (years of research, for example), but looking at architecture for clues is far from the worst. You will discover that many of Russia's buildings reveal the contradictions alive in the society itself.

For the purposes of this book, Russia's "enigma" is its creative core, the process by which it absorbs and adapts foreign influences to its own unique ends. And the "riddle" is the inaccessible language, both the spoken and the visual product of the enigma. As you walk, we will draw your attention to many details familiar from other cultures. But it is important not to be deceived by surfaces. Even Western-looking Leningrad was built according to the dictates of absolutism. In the United States the architectural precedents of Greece and Rome were exploited to house the ideal republic. In St. Petersburg the same idiom served as propaganda for an "enlightened," yet absolute, monarch. As early as the fifteenth century, Muscovy borrowed styles from early-Renaissance Italy, but it would be hard to mistake Kremlin churches for their counterparts in the Latin states.

Russiawalks combines maps and clear instructions on where to go, and "walking essays" in which streets and buildings are brought to life through historical background, legends, and the personalities associated with them. Instead of a dull array of dates and names, we have tried to place what you will see in colorful context.

We cover both Moscow and Leningrad, thereby providing a historical continuum. Three of the four Moscow walks evoke the pre-Petrine Era, before Leningrad (originally St. Petersburg) had even been born. The first Moscow walk will take us to the oldest and most revealing sector of the city, the Kremlin; the second walk will cover an area that developed slightly later, Red Square and Kitai Gorod; and on the third walk we will visit Novodyevichi Convent, one of the richest monasteries in Russia, which reached its baroque zenith just before Peter the Great took power. The fourth Moscow walk takes us down streets whose buildings evoke the nineteenth century, after St. Petersburg had established itself as the country's political center.

Leningrad, which constitutes the second half of this book, evolved in such a compressed period of time that its walks will emphasize the city's different architectural modes rather than separate historical epochs. In the fifth walk, we will take in the meaning of the city's vistas and ensembles; in the sixth walk, we will see how parks and gardens are fluidly incorporated into the urban scheme; and in the seventh walk we will witness the effect of the vast Neva River on the grand palaces of its embankment. All three walks will reveal the city's classical essence, and will take us down charming interior riverways and canals, the reason the city has often been described as the "Venice of the North." And all three give good excuses for historical anecdotes and royal gossip.

Many of today's political disputes have their roots in the distant past. While we do not suggest that our walks will provide answers to these conflicts, at least the shape of the enigma and the sound of the riddle should become clearer. We refer to the Kremlin as "a map to the Russian psyche, a hieroglyph to be deciphered," which is a good way to think of all these walks. Our hope is that, rather than a giddy swirl of exotic impressions, your trip to Russia will lead to a clearer and better-informed delight.

Information
and Advice

Traveling in the Soviet Union is not at all like knocking about Western Europe. Though there is more flexibility today than perhaps ever before, the country does not make improvisation in travel easy. As much as possible must be planned ahead of time. Russia can be endlessly fascinating, and we intend to guide you well, but first understand that you must accept the parameters laid out below.

VISAS

Not only do you require a visa, but each city you hope to visit has to be listed on your visa application along with the dates you plan to be there. Resist the sudden impulse to visit Sverdlovsk when your visa lists only Moscow, Leningrad, and Vladimir-Suzdal as destinations. Given how easy it is to obtain permission to travel where you want anyway, it doesn't make sense to take risks. For extensions of or changes to your itinerary once you have reached the Soviet Union, contact the Intourist bureau in your hotel.

You are probably best off making your visa application through a travel agent or Intourist itself. They are the best sources of application forms. If you choose to submit your visa application yourself, it should be sent to:

Consular Division
Embassy of the USSR
1825 Phelps Place, N.W.
Washington, D.C. 20008
Tel. 202/332-1513

In Canada the address is:

Consular Division
Embassy of the USSR
52 Range Road
Ottawa, Ontario
Tel. 613/236-7220

In England the address is:

Consular Division
Embassy of the USSR
5 Kensington Palace Gardens
London W8
Tel. 071/727-6888

You will need to provide proof of a place to stay (such as a confirmed hotel reservation) for each destination before your visa will be granted. Make sure to submit your application six to eight weeks in advance of planned departure.

If you are making a personal visit on the invitation of family members or friends, a special visitor's visa application must be accompanied by a formal invitation from them. Your hosts can obtain this document in the Soviet Union from the Department of Visas and Registration (Upravleniya Viz I Registratsiya), known as UVIR This government department has offices in all major cities down to *raion* (district) capitals. Regular mail from the Soviet Union can take months to arrive, so they should choose a more reliable method of transmitting the invitation to you (such as a new Soviet international mail service that takes one week, or a mutual acquaintance who happens to be traveling).

Visa and travel regulations may well change in coming months. Make sure that you follow the most current procedures as you make your plans. Again, either Intourist or a good travel agent can help you.

INTOURIST AND OTHER AGENCIES

Intourist is the government agency responsible for most tourist travel (for both locals and foreigners) in the Soviet Union. Whether or not you are part of a tour, you or your travel agent will have to make arrangements with Intourist for hotel accommodations and internal travel, unless you make use of one of the alternatives we describe below. Intourist's main offices in North America and Britain are as follows:

United States:
630 Fifth Avenue, Suite 868
New York, N.Y. 10111
Tel. 212/757-3884

Canada:
1801 McGill College Avenue
Montreal, Quebec H3A 2N4
Tel. 514/849-6394

United Kingdom:
Intourist House, Meridian Gate
Marsh Wall, London E14
Tel. 01/538-5902

The only cases in which you would not have contact with Intourist would be if you had a private invitation, booked your flight directly, and did not stay in any hotels; or if you made your arrangements through one of a handful of firms that specialize in finding space in private homes or bed-and-breakfasts.

For a long time Intourist has had a monopoly on tourist travel in the Soviet Union, and over the years there have been complaints about service: from dilapidated hotel rooms to unappealing food to uninformative guides. However, in recent years hotels up to international standards have been built, and their restaurants are at least making an effort. Another hopeful sign is the emergence of competition, which may force Intourist to push harder to accommodate the wishes of its clients. The advantage of being a monopoly has been that travelers had nowhere to turn with their dollars. There are still few alternatives, but the number of private firms catering to the tourist industry in the Soviet Union is growing.

Especially if one of your objectives is to meet Russians, then you might consider an end run around Intourist. The following agencies are pioneers:

Travelling Shoes, at Box 4410, Laguna Beach, Calif. 92652; tel. 714/497-6773, offers several programs, all of which involve living with screened, English-speaking Russian families. A two-week visit to Moscow and Leningrad, which includes accommodations, meals, transportation, touring, and several evenings at the opera, ballet, or theater, costs around $1,400 (round-trip airfare to the Soviet Union is not included in the price). Travelling Shoes also has a program for professionals, which allows them to meet with their Soviet counterparts.

Amico, Intl., at 13113 Ideal Drive, Silver Spring, Md. 20906; tel. 301/942-3770, offers bed-and-breakfast accommodations in Moscow, Leningrad, Kiev, Tallin, Vilnius, Riga, Tbilisi, and Tashkent at $75 a night for a single and $85 a night for a double. The hosts all speak English and can help the visitor find tour guides and whatever else he or she might need. Amico can also arrange the renting of efficiency apartments in many of these cities.

If you are planning a longer stay in Moscow, you might want to rent your own apartment. Make sure in doing so that you have someone with you who has experience in Moscow. When it comes to housing in the capital, it's a dog-eat-dog world. You will find almost incomprehensible variations in price. In some instances you will be permitted to pay rubles, although usually the rule is dollars. The following Moscow-based agencies might be able to help you: Jupiter at 250-2300, Astoria at 229-2300, Rubin at 283-1659, and Avangard at 455-9210.

Does the idea of scaling the frozen Pamir Mountains on the Afghan border or biking the ancient Silk Route to China tickle you? For more outlandish tours, contact Bill Dawson at R.E.I. Adventure Travel, P. O. Box 88126, Seattle, Wash. 98138; tel. 206/395-3780.

Local officials in tourist regions have also begun to act, largely because they want some of the hard currency foreigners bring with them. In Vladimir-Suzdal, for example, the local soviet (governing council) has expelled Intourist and has taken over administration of local hotels and tours. The result has been a higher level of service and guides who are very well informed about history, architecture, and art. Intourist can still make the arrangements in Vladimir and Suzdal for you; the difference is that they do not provide the services themselves. Municipal officials from Leningrad to Vladivostok are now examining how they can benefit from tourism. It is a trend for which we should be grateful.

As an individual traveler, beware. The Soviet tourism bureaucracy was not set up to serve you. For a certain type of daring person, problems away from home are an adventure; for other connoisseurs of architecture and culture, anything that interferes is a disappointment. You can run into problems as an individual, particularly when trying first to reach and then to gain entry into famous churches and museums, especially in the afternoon when tickets may have "run out." Groups led by official guides do not face these barriers. (Luckily, tickets to the Kremlin cathedrals are almost never a problem, and easy access is typical of most of the museums on our walks.) Even if you are not part of a package tour, you can always hire a guide or join a group to visit any particular monument, and this is often a solution to the friction of travel alone.

You can book local tours; purchase ballet, opera, concert, and theater tickets; and make restaurant reservations through the service bureau in your hotel. Otherwise, make use of your host (if you are staying in a bed-and-breakfast) or other Russian contact to make such arrangements.

Another solution, if you have deep pockets, is to book an individual tour through Intourist for which you can set your own itinerary. You will be supplied with a car, driver, guide, and sometimes translator. Naturally, the more they give you the more it costs.

While we do not encourage spontaneity in travel plans, we very much encourage it once you have arrived where you said you were going. Doing certain things on your own can be less expensive (and frankly, more informative) than doing them with Intourist. Keep in mind that Intourist guides cleared to work with foreigners are required to report on their groups. Unusual or illicit behavior that is observed will quickly reach the files of the secret police. Occasionally, Intourist's guides are very knowledgeable. In that event, stick by him or her because a good guide can be a fountain of information and will gladly answer questions. Other tour leaders range from the mediocre on down, in which case you are better off compensating by doing even more on your own. Needless to say, each walk is preceded by instructions on how to get to the starting point.

If you are determined, there are ways of coming into contact with "real" Russians, but it may be at the price of comfort and predictability. Intourist will reliably and painlessly cart you to the major tourist sites, and if you are lucky the guide will know some history. What you choose should depend on your temperament.

HOTELS

No matter how eager local officials are to attract visitors, and how welcoming Russians are by nature, there remains a serious obstacle. Virtually every Soviet city is plagued by a shortage of hotel rooms. A number of Soviet and Western companies are planning to rectify this situation, and we can hope that in several years the supply of good rooms in major cities will begin to meet demand. Until then, you should take accommodations just as seriously as getting a visa. Don't count on being able to extend your stay in Moscow or Leningrad by several days. You might be given a flat "*Nyet*," or at the very least be forced to change rooms.

As a foreigner you may not walk into a Soviet hotel and register. You are restricted to those hotels set aside for foreigners, which usually require reservations well in advance. The service you will receive is far higher than what local people get, even if it does not meet the standards of the West.

You will notice on entering that you run a gauntlet of youths offering to change money, meaty taxi drivers, and officious doormen. It is unfortunate that hotels seem to attract a stratum of society that most reputable Russians look on with contempt: black marketeers and mafiosi-types. The doormen are there to keep ordinary Russians out, all the while allowing the unpleasant ones to ply their trade. You may bring accompanied guests in with you, although they will probably have to register if you take them up to your room. Hotels are not a good place for romantic trysts.

Hotel security does have a reassuring side. Twenty-four hours a day on each floor is usually seated an elderly woman with a good view of the corridor and elevators, who keeps track of everyone who enters or leaves her domain. She will take your key when you leave and give it back when you return. You can request tea, fresh linen, and other amenities from her. A *dezhurnaya* can be intimidatingly gruff, but try being nice or giving her a small gift, and you may discover a streak of sentimentality.

Aside from your room and the restaurant, the most important place in the hotel is the Intourist bureau, or in smaller hotels, simply the service bureau. Unless you speak Russian, it is the service bureau that can best make arrangements for you to get about the city. Use as much charm as you can to get whoever is sitting at the desk to like you. They are often busy and harrassed; don't be offended at brusqueness, but remain sturdily polite and insistent. It can make a big difference to your trip.

If you fall in love with Moscow, discover that you asked for far too little time, and lose your room to an onslaught of new tourists, there is still hope. Try one of the following recently established joint-venture or cooperative hotels:

The Flamingo (a hotel on a boat), at 255-9278 or
 253-9578
Hotel Vizit, at 202-2848
Novoye Vremya, at 274-4694 or 274-1089

Above all, use your hotel as a base. Leave in the morning and if possible come back only late at night. Don't get hung up on service or what is or isn't provided. After all, you're in the hotel to see Russia, not vice versa.

RESTAURANTS AND CAFÉS

You will likely spend plenty of time downing hotel fare in the course of your stay. All the more reason to get out and experience a phenomenon that is truly a product of the Gorbachev era: "cooperative" cafés.

It is now de rigueur for visitors to Russia to eat at privately owned establishments. Not only are the service and food usually better than in state-run restaurants, but you also become witness to a phenomenon peculiar to Gorbachev-era Russia. The lists we offer at the end of the book cover primarily such cooperative cafés, with a few older and more traditional eating spots included.

When you visit a cooperative, understand first that the Russian patrons you will be seeing are not run-of-the-mill. Even if the restaurant accepts rubles, the prices are so high that only the wealthiest Russians can afford them. For this reason, cooperatives arouse great emotion. Conservatives and common people complain bitterly about the high prices, and their anger smolders in the belief, sometimes justified, that private enterprises sell goods gained through theft or favoritism, which would otherwise be available in the state system of controlled prices. The upshot is that customers are Soviets entertaining foreigners officially, black marketeers, or members of the tiny group that is getting rich off legitimate private enterprise.

Here are some further pointers:

Make reservations. Many of the best restaurants are popular and you cannot count on getting a table just by walking in. Also, be aware that many restaurants divide their clientele into those paying hard (convertible) currency, like dollars, and those not. There is rarely a difference in service, but ruble reservations are harder to come by. Specify how you intend to pay when you make your reservation to avoid confusion later on.

Always try to pay in rubles, since the new tourist exchange rate of approximately twenty-seven rubles to the dollar is much better than the rate you will be charged if you use a credit card. Be prepared for pressure on this issue. If the restaurant claims that it will take either rubles or hard currency, just stick to your guns. Also be aware if you are planning to use hard currency that most restaurants are not allowed to take cash. You generally must use a credit card.

Be sure to include *zakuski* (appetizers), both hot and cold, in your meal. They are a large and traditional part of Russian cuisine, and as much attention goes into their preparation as into the main dishes. As a general rule you should order caviar (*ee-KRAH*), mushrooms (*gree-BEE*), thin pancakes (*blee-NEE*), sturgeon (*ah-SYO-ter*), and any special salads, meat, or fish dishes the waiter recommends.

Many restaurants will not sell liquor for rubles (they argue that they must pay hard currency to obtain it), and in any event the selection is usually very limited. You are almost always better off bringing your wine, vodka, or cognac with you (liquor is easily available in hard currency Beriozka stores). If the waiter objects to the procedure, slip him a few extra rubles.

If you are the sort that likes coffee or tea after a meal, don't count on the restaurant's having it, even for hard currency. Take your coffee or tea with you (it also is easily available in the Beriozkas), and if at the end of the meal the waiter tells you there is none, simply ask for boiling water (*kee-pyah-TOK*) and cups (*CHASH-kee*), and make your own.

A 15 percent tip is standard, although some restaurants add it in automatically as a not-always-evident service charge. Don't be bashful about asking whether it was included. In theory, state-run restaurants don't expect patrons to tip. As is so often the case, theory rarely corresponds with practice. Tip anyway.

Any cooperative you visit is an economic experiment, and it provides insight into Russia's unfolding adventure. Go at least once to see *perestroika* in progress.

SHOPPING

The Soviet Union is not thought of as a shopper's paradise, but you will be surprised at what you can find if you nose around a bit. While we all read about the shortages, items that are available rarely make the news. The Soviet economy is huge and many items are inexpensive by our standards. Keep your eyes peeled particularly for ceramics, glassware, crystal, amber or semiprecious stone jewelry, clothing, fabrics, kitchen implements, tableware, and traditional crafts.

Our listing at the back of the book includes three basic categories of stores: hard-currency stores that sell everything from goblets to groceries; commission stores that sell, for rubles, valuables on consignment like furniture, paintings, and jewelry; and ruble stores of all kinds that average Russians use.

It is easiest and least time consuming to use hard-currency stores, especially Beriozkas, which have preselected items of interest to tourists that are often unavailable in the other stores. You pay a premium for this convenience. In Beriozkas all prices are marked in rubles, but you pay in hard currency (cash or credit cards) at the old rate of $1.62 to the ruble, many times less favorable than the current tourist rate.

Nevertheless, Beriozkas are well worth visiting, and even at the inflated exchange rate, worthwhile buys can be found. Often they are the only places to get cigarettes, liquor, coffee, and tea, all of which, by the way, make welcome hostess gifts if you receive an invitation to visit a Russian at home. The other advantage of Beriozkas is that all your purchases there are exportable. Just be sure to have your purchase receipt with you when you pass through customs.

Commission stores are a trickier business, in part because you have to look harder for a buy, but also because you can run afoul of export regulations. For even exportable items duties can run as high as 100 percent when you have paid for them in rubles.

The same warnings that apply to commission stores apply to ruble stores, only it is more difficult to find items of real value. Pay special heed to clothing stores. Heavy winter coats can sometimes be an extraordinary buy, as can all sorts of fabrics, glassware, and crystal (when you can find it). But beware of duties, or an outright ban on export. Any item with the patina of age risks confiscation on your way out. If you plan to shop, pay special attention to the following remarks on customs.

CUSTOMS

Make a complete customs declaration when you enter the country. You should be given the form on the airplane before you land. This should include all the cash, travelers checks, expensive electronic gear, and precious and semiprecious jewelry you are carrying (don't forget your wedding band). Be thorough. It would be unfortunate to have something confiscated on your way out because you can't prove you brought it into the country. Don't pad the declaration with items you hope to buy: customs officers will check to see that you are indeed carrying what you say. The form will be stamped, and you will keep it until you depart the country.

Keep all the receipts you receive for changing your dollars, pounds, marks, or other convertible currency into rubles. This will enable you to change leftover rubles back before you leave. You will be expected to hand over these receipts along with your customs declaration when you depart. If there is a major discrepancy in the money you are carrying, and you cannot document how it was legally obtained, the excess may very well be confiscated.

Make sure to hang onto receipts for the purchase of items in Beriozkas or other hard-currency stores. The receipts guarantee your right to export and exempt you from any duties.

The Soviets are very serious about protecting their cultural patrimony from export, and some of the rules seem almost excessively tough. For example, it is not permitted to export any book published before 1977, or any "antique" (painting, chair, necklace, or bibelot) dated before 1945. It is possible to obtain exceptions from an export office in Moscow at 29 Chekhov Street (a walk from the Mayakovsky Metro station), open Tuesdays from 10:00 until 2:00. Forget about anything that truly qualifies as an antique, or for pre-Revolutionary book editions. For smuggling you risk confiscation, or if the contraband is of great value (like diamonds or a medieval icon), prison.

The irony in attempting to export artwork is that you would probably be risking everything for a fake. Few people are aware that Moscow is a center of high-quality forgeries of everything from icons to early twentieth-century modernist paintings and prints.

HEALTH

To call an ambulance, dial 03.

Contrary to the advice in some other guidebooks, the tap water in Moscow and Leningrad is not safe to drink. Many have come down with an intestinal parasite, *Giardia lamblia*, that causes mild to acute discomfort and is difficult to purge.

In general, fresh fruits and vegetables (when you see them) are safe when peeled or washed in boiled water, and you rarely have to be squeamish about cooked foods. Shortly after the Chernobyl explosion in 1986, there were rumors about mushrooms showing residual radiation as far north as the Arctic Circle, and picking them was discouraged by the government. Mushrooms are a delicious element of Russian cuisine, and five years later there should be little danger. In 1987 the U.S. State Department reported that "levels of radiation in food items affected from the Chernobyl accident have decreased significantly with time. They are no longer of any known medical significance to the traveler." This, of course, does not apply to the Chernobyl region, or to heavily contaminated areas of the Ukraine and Byelorussia.

We strongly advise not getting sick in the Soviet Union. Although health care is ostensibly free—although you would be mad not to bribe your doctor and every nurse in sight if you wind up in a hospital—the system is literally disintegrating. Family and friends usually watch over patients around the clock; these shifts feed and bathe the patients, and change the sheets. They also dispense "presents" to ensure that doctors and nurses are attentive at critical moments.

If you feel seriously ill, have the hotel administrator (assuming you are in a hotel) call for an ambulance or a doctor. The response will be much faster than if simply anyone were to call. There are special Soviet clinics for foreigners that offer slightly better care than ordinary facilities. The administrator would normally instruct the driver to head to one of these clinics:

In Moscow, on Dobrinsky Pereulok 4 (near the Dobrinsky Metro station on the Brown Circle Line). The telephone number is 237-5933 or 237-5395 for emergencies.

In Moscow, at 12 Herzen Street (Ulitsa Gertsena). Its telephone numbers are 229-7323 and 229-0382.

In Leningrad, the clinic for foreigners is on Moskovsky Prospect. Any doctor or ambulance driver will know where it is.

In Moscow there is also a French-run private hospital, International Health Care, at Gruzinsky Pereulok 3, Building 2, which is open by appointment for hard currency. The telephone numbers are 253-0703 and 253-0704.

Bring ample supplies of any medications you require, since Western pharmaceuticals are hard to obtain in the

Soviet Union. Anything that could be classed as a narcotic should be accompanied by a letter from your doctor, or you risk problems with customs. There are several places in Moscow where you can buy some Western brand-name drugs for hard currency: on the second floor of the Mezhdunarodnaya Hotel; at Unipharm, which is located at 13 Skatertny Pereulok (tel. 202-5071); and on the outskirts of the city at Beskudnekovsky Bulvar 59a (tel. 905-4227).

If your condition is serious, try to leave the country. Many foreigners in Moscow fly to Finland or Germany for medical procedures. You might want to take out a medical evacuation insurance policy for the duration of your trip. Your travel agent can recommend carriers.

MAIL

Incoming mail for tourists in the Soviet Union should be addressed c/o Intourist, if possible in Russian. Even if you write in English, try to follow the traditional Russian address format, which is almost the exact reverse of English practice. The top line is the country of destination; the second line is the city and a regional code; the third line is the street address; and the fourth line is the name of the addressee (last name first). The return address is usually located below the main address in the center of the envelope, although Russians sometimes place it in the upper left corner, as we do. This advice should come in handy if you correspond with Soviet citizens as well.

Mail for tourists in Moscow should be addressed as follows, with the Russian added as an encouragement:

USSR
Moscow K-600
Tverskaya Street 3–5
c/o Intourist
Last Name, First Name

For Leningrad the address reads:

> USSR
> Leningrad C-400
> Nevsky Prospect 6
> c/o Intourist
> Last Name, First Name

It is also a good idea to add somewhere on the envelope the expected date of arrival of the tourist recipient. Mail will be held at the above two locations until the addressee comes for it. Do keep in mind that international mail in and out of the Soviet Union is notoriously slow and unreliable, so don't break off an engagement over a missed letter, especially if you happen to be, say, a Pentagon official.

For mail originating in the Soviet Union, stamps are very easy to come by at any of the numerous street kiosks that sell newspapers; tobacco; bus, trolleybus, and tram tickets; and other odds and ends.

To mail parcels either overseas or internally, you must visit a post office where an attendant examines the contents before packing them himself in a standard cardboard box. There is a maximum weight limit of 10 kilos (22 pounds) for each parcel.

Outgoing mail to the United States need not be addressed in Russian, but you might want to write "USA" in Cyrillic letters (**США**) to make clear the destination to postal personnel.

Several international express mail companies now have offices in Moscow including:

> Federal Express
> 12 Krasnopesnenskaya Naberezhnaya
> Moscow 123610
> USSR
> Tel. 253-1641

DHL
1 Ulitsa Vesnina
Moscow 119034
USSR
Tel. 201-2585 and 202-8090

Federal Express, for example, can get a document to the United States in two business days for sixty-five dollars including pickup. Packages take longer and cost more. Keep in mind that service for both companies is in hard currency only, and that express mail originating overseas can be delivered only to business or official addresses in the Soviet Union.

TELEPHONE

Emergency numbers, which require no coins from pay phones, are as follows:

Fire	01
Police	02
Ambulance	03

Local calls in either Moscow or Leningrad made from a telephone booth cost the princely sum of 2 kopecks (a fraction of a cent). The procedure is to place either a 2-kopeck or two 1-kopeck coins in the slot at the top of the telephone and to dial. When the connection is made the coins will automatically drop into the box; if there is no answer or the line is busy, you can fish your coins out of the slot.

Long-distance telephone calls within the Soviet Union follow a similar procedure, only the special phone booths labeled *mezhdugorodny* (**междугородный**), meaning "between city," are rarer, you have to add an area code to the number, and the calls cost fifteen kopecks. Moscow's area code is 095; Leningrad's is 012. Most such long-distance phones have charts posted listing codes for across the country.

International telephone calls can be very expensive. Several hotels offer direct dial from special phone booths, which require purchase of cards for hard currency ahead of time. Otherwise, you can place the call through the hotel operator. Unless you can bill someone else for the call, watch out! It will take a real bite out of your wallet. Nor should you ever promise someone overseas that you will call at a specific time. It sometimes takes hours to get a clear circuit, although the situation has somewhat improved recently.

You may also order international calls from certain telegraph and telephone stations, for which you are allowed to pay rubles. Unfortunately, you often have to book your slot hours or days in advance.

The address of Moscow's Central Telegraph and Telephone is Tverskaya Ulitsa 19, very near the center of town. It is open from 8:00 A.M. until 11:30 P.M., with last bookings at 10:30. Leningrad's central station is at Ulitsa Gertsena 3–5, just off Nevsky Prospect and almost adjacent to the Empire archway leading to Palace Square.

You can also place international calls from private apartments, a very frustrating undertaking. The operator will often answer that there is no space for several days; several days later, the answer is the same, and so on. Communications is one area in which the Soviet Union remains at a primitive level. However, the country has been increasing the number of international circuits and the waiting time is beginning to diminish.

TRANSPORTATION

Transportation about the major cities of the Soviet Union is relatively easy. The mass transit system is efficient, well developed, and extremely inexpensive. Both Moscow and

Leningrad have clean and attractive subway systems, which is the preferred method of getting around the two cities. At the start of each walk we identify the metro stop that is most appropriate to use.

Entry into either subway system now costs fifteen kopecks. You deposit a coin in the turnstile and pass through, just as you use subway tokens in Boston and New York. Until recently, the fare was five kopecks, and the large bronze-colored coins in that denomination were used for entry. Assuming they keep the old system, numerous change machines at every entryway will allow you to break larger coins into 15-kopeck pieces. Knowledge of the Cyrillic alphabet is invaluable when you are underground, if only to decipher which stop you've arrived at. Maps of both systems are easily available locally at newspaper kiosks. Just ask for *"plahn metro"* (map of the metro). Moscow's subway is open from 6:00 A.M. to 1:00 A.M. every day, while Leningrad's opens a half-hour earlier and closes at the same time.

Moscow's system has the added advantage of being especially beautiful. Built throughout the terrible 1930s, no expense was spared to present an idyllic vision of Soviet life under socialism. Mosaics, tilework, frescoes, elaborate plaster, bronze sculpture, and marble and granite sheathing decorate the underground stations. Farms at harvest, soldiers in battle, and the proletariat at work are imaged throughout. Intourist even offers a tour that will lead you to the stops most famous for their elaborate decoration.

Buses, trolleybuses, and trams are equally reliable even if rickety in appearance and motion. They are difficult for the short-term visitor to use, simply because the routes are more complex than the easily decipherable subway map. Once upon a time the tickets for each mode of surface transport were different: now the same 15-kopeck ticket (not a coin, as in the metro) applies to all. You can buy these tickets at the ubiquitous kiosks, usually in packets of ten. If you board a bus without a ticket, you can often buy five or ten from the driver himself when he stops at a light. The procedure is to tear off one of the tickets, and punch it full of holes in a stamp provided for that purpose. When your car is crowded, just hand your ticket to a neighbor in the direction of the stamp: he will pass it on to be stamped, and it follows the same route back to you. If you take up position next to a stamping machine on a crowded bus, be prepared to do a lot of ticket punching. Even if you're in the middle of the car, a tap on the shoulder is usually a sign that your neighbor wants you to pass a ticket on.

The honor system prevails: it is possible to board a bus without a ticket. But beware of *kontrol*, ladies who board to check each passenger's ticket (they can tell by the pattern of holes if you are reusing an old ticket). The fine for traveling without a ticket is 10 rubles plus the 15-kopeck fare. If you don't have the fine, get ready for a trip to the police station.

Taxis are another story altogether. In Moscow the old taxi service hardly functions. The rare taxi driver that does stop, or whom you find outside your foreigners' hotel, will almost invariably demand dollars at extortionate rates. American cigarettes are no longer the incentive they once were, so forget the stories you've heard about waving packages of Marlboros or flaunting Beriozka bags. For Russians it is virtually impossible to get a taxi. It is better not to rely even on taxis ordered ahead of time to take you to important appointments or to the airport. Sometimes they simply don't show up.

The prevailing explanation is that Moscow's taxi stands are controlled by organized crime and the drivers are busy delivering contraband like moonshine liquor. Drivers simply have much better things to do than waste their time picking up passengers. If you do get a cab, check the meter when you get in, since drivers often neglect to turn them off between fares. Usually, however, the meter is not an issue because the fare will have been negotiated beforehand. Our advice is that you forget the word *taxi* for the duration of your stay in Moscow.

In Leningrad it is still possible to get taxis. The city seems to be at about the stage Moscow was three or four years ago. Bribes are often requested, but sometimes drivers actually pick you up and drive by the meter. Simply out of gratitude you should double or triple the official fare. The rates are so low that little damage will be done to your wallet.

If you stand by the side of the road with your arm up, unmarked cars of private citizens often will stop. While we do not recommend them, many veteran residents of Moscow and Leningrad travel this way. Sometimes the fare is negotiated (minuscule in comparison to what taxi drivers want), and sometimes nary a word other than destination is uttered. In the latter case the client is expected discreetly to leave behind money for the driver. Three to five rubles is the going day rate, and up to ten at night. Or a package of American cigarettes is often a welcome gift. The risks of such travel are obvious and the legality doubtful. Women alone should not even consider traveling this way.

CLIMATE

May through September are the best months to visit Moscow and Leningrad, although the advantages of the off season include less-expensive tours and nights at the ballet and opera, which are then in season. Unless you find severe cold bracing, Russian winters can be harsh for casual strolling. In January, Moscow's average temperatures hover in the low teens and can drop far lower. Leningrad is usually a few degrees warmer, but you can be cut through by a bitter wind off the Neva River.

If you plan a summer trip to Leningrad, you might try to make it in June, during the White Nights of the summer solstice, when the sun never sets on the city and the baroque buildings glow in silver gray. Summers in Moscow can be idyllic also. Temperatures go as high as the 80s Fahrenheit, but almost never into the 90s. Summer nights in both cities can be cool, so be sure to pack a couple of sweaters and a light raincoat even if you plan to travel in July or August. Needless to say, winter demands heavy winter clothing and good boots. But some days break clear and lovely with temperatures in the high 20s or 30s, perfect for walking.

As a city on the coast, Leningrad gets heavy precipitation, and fall and spring (particularly November, March, and April) can be marred by weeks of chilling rain. If you have to make a choice between late fall and winter, you are better off with the white season in both cities.

BLACK MARKET

Don't change money on the black market or purchase items on the street for dollars. You will without question be accosted by *fartsovshiki* (black marketeers) offering to change money, and street vendors will sometimes insist on payment in *valuta* (hard currency). The rate of exchange typically offered can not be much better than the official rate (now at 27 rubles to the dollar). If large amounts of money are involved you run the risk of being cheated or robbed.

In any event, you should avoid the temptation of trying to stretch your dollars. People do get arrested for these transactions by plainclothesmen surveilling the popular outdoor markets. The same goes for the sale of electronic items, computers, and clothing.

Statistics suggest that street crime in Soviet cities has increased significantly, and anecdotal evidence supports the impression. Foreigners are a tempting target because they are presumed to be carrying convertible currency. Even so, Moscow and Leningrad are not nearly as dangerous as large American cities. Use the same common sense and caution that is called for in major cities the world over: don't flaunt jewelry; avoid deserted streets late at night; and stay away from groups of rowdy-looking youths. Involving yourself in black-market transactions can make you vulnerable. To the extent that you are permitted to spend rubles, the Soviet Union is already a bargain. Don't jeopardize your trip by getting greedy.

READING

Read about Russia before you go. It is impossible to exaggerate how much your pleasure is increased when you know what you are looking at. This book is designed to make you an informed and intelligent tourist, but nothing can compensate for a reading program prior to the trip. Some guides offer reading lists, but the subject of Russian history, not to mention literature, is so immense that even the longest list would be incomplete. You might want to use the bibliography of this book as a starting point, and then follow idiosyncratic whim.

George Vernadsky's multivolume history of Russia is a standard English text, and has been condensed into a one-volume edition; that might be a good place to start. There is a recent and vividly written one-volume history of the Romanovs from 1613 through the Revolution by W. Bruce Lincoln. The book is a pleasure to read, but Lincoln at times bends far to treat his monarchs sympathetically. And be sure to include some juicy memoirs in your reading. Catherine the Great's autobiography is a classic in a genre in which Russia is rich indeed, and gives an unforgettable impression of royal life in eighteenth-century St. Petersburg. The French Marquis de Custine described the essence of Nicholas I's despotism in his classic travel account, *Russia in 1839*. For a disturbing portrait of the Stalin era, try Nadezhda Mandelstam's *Hope Against Hope*. These are only a few suggestions; the subject is vast. You cannot hope to cover it all, so you might as well read what most appeals to you. Almost any memoir or history will lead to a payoff, when you find yourself in front of a palace or church to which you can attach a remembered story.

RUSSIAN

It would also be well worth your while to learn the thirty-three letters of the Russian alphabet. The language is highly phonetic, so simply knowing the sounds will allow you to spell out street names, a great boon to foot-loose adventure. If you have time, buy one of those one- or two-week courses in Russian on tape. A little bit of effort will go a long way. To encourage you, we have included some useful phrases for you at the end of this guide.

CHANGING NAMES

Russia's ongoing political revolution means chaos for mapmakers. Names of many cities, streets, squares, ponds, and buildings are being restored to their pre-Bolshevik Revolution originals. In general, we have tried to offer both old and new names, with whichever one is officially out of use in parentheses.

Moscow has taken the lead in wholesale name-changing. In 1990, in what was a clear smack at the Communists, the City Council voted on the eve of the Anniversary of the Russian Revolution to rename twenty-two major streets, six squares, and ten metro stations. The changes are said to be final and cannot be overturned by any other governmental body. The City Council plans to exhibit the statues and art work removed from sites named for Bolshevik heroes in a soon-to-be established Museum of Totalitarianism.

Some of the changes, which include most of Moscow's major avenues, are as follows:

SQUARES AND PONDS
  Fiftieth Anniversary of October - Manezhnaya
  Sverdlova - Teatralnaya
  Dzerzhinskaya - Lubyanskaya

Kolkhoznaya and Malaya Kolkhoznaya -
  Sukharevskaya
Belorusskogo Vokzala - Tverskaya Zastava
Pioneer Ponds - Patriarch Ponds

STREETS

Kuibysheva - Ilinka
Razina - Varvarka
Kalinina - Vozdvizhenka
Prospect Kalinina - Noviy Arbat
Dzerzhinskogo - Bolshaya Lubyanka
Frunze - Znamenka
Kirova - Myasnitskaya
Bolshaya Khmelnitskaya - Maroseika
Kropotkinskaya - Prechistenka
Gorkogo:
    (from Mokhovaya to Mayakovskaya Square) -
      Tverskaya
    (from Mayakovskaya Square to Tverskaya Zastava) -
      Pervaya Tverskaya Yamskaya
Karla Marksa - Staraya Basmannaya
Tchaikovskogo - Novinskiy Boulevard
Dobryninskaya - Koroviy Val
Suslova - Aminevskoye Shosse
Ustinova - Osenniy Bulvar
Valtera Ulbrikhta - Novopeschanaya
Georgiu Dezha - Vtoraya Peschanaya
Prospect Marksa:
    (from Manege to Moskva Hotel) - Mokhovaya
    (from Moskva Hotel to Teatralnaya Square) -
      Okhotniy Ryad
    (from Teatralnaya Square to Lubyankaya Square) -
      Teatralniy Proezd

METRO STATIONS

Gorkovskaya - Tverskaya
Prospekt Marksa - Okhotniy Ryad
Ploshad' Sverdlova - Teatralnaya

Ploshad' Nogina - Kitai Gorod
Kalininskaya - Vozdvizhenskaya
Dzerzhinskaya - Lubyanskaya
Kirovskaya - Myasnitskaya
Kolkhoznaya - Sukharevskaya
Shcherbakovskaya - Novoalekseyevskaya
Lenina - Aleksino

Leningrad is in the midst of a debate as to whether or not to change its name back to St. Petersburg. We asked the liberal mayor, Anatoly Sobchak, when this might occur and he answered that if we covered the expense, he would do it "tomorrow." The question was supposed to have been decided by referendum in March 1991, but a vote has been put off. A restoration of the old name is likely at some point, but no one knows when. Expense is a deterrent, as is the opposition of the older generation, who associate the current name with the heroic defense of the city during World War II, as well as with the Bolshevik Revolution itself.

Two ancient centers of Russian culture, the cities of Gorky and Kalinin, have already had their traditional names restored to Nizhni Novgorod and Tver, respectively. This renaming is a process likely to continue for years, outdating maps almost as soon as they are produced.

MOSCOW
WALKS

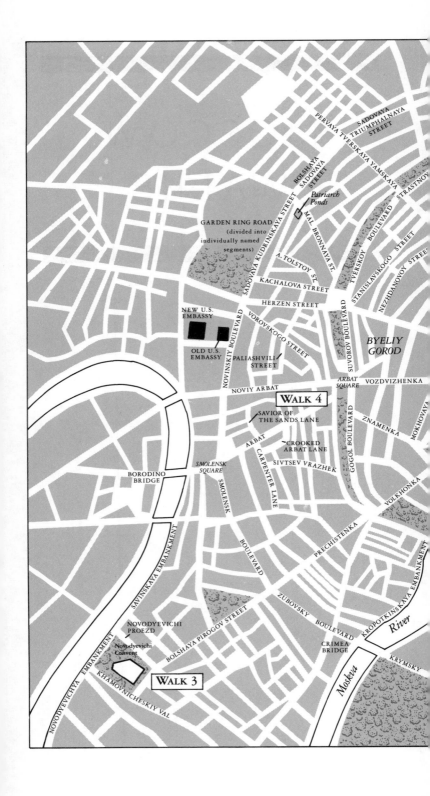

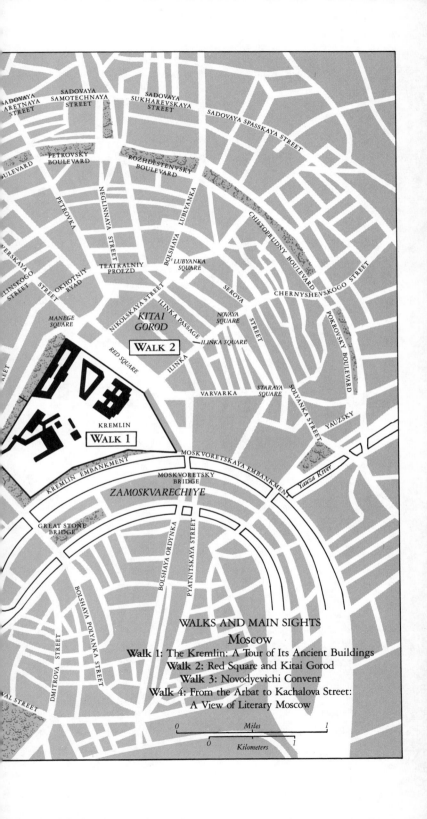

SADOVAYA KARETNAYA STREET

SADOVAYA SAMOTECHNAYA STREET

SADOVAYA SUKHAREVSKAYA STREET

SADOVAYA SPASSKAYA STREET

PETROVSKY BOULEVARD

BOULEVARD

ROZHDESTENVSKY BOULEVARD

PETROVKA

NEGLINNAYA STREET

CHISTOPRUDNY BOULEVARD

VERSKAYA STREET

ELINSKOGO STREET

OKHOTNIY RYAD

TEATRALNIY PROEZD

BOLSHAYA LUBYANKA

LUBYANKA SQUARE

SEROVA

CHERNYSHEVSKOGO STREET

NIKOLSKAYA STREET

MANEGE SQUARE

KITAI GOROD

ILINKA PASSAGE

NOVAYA SQUARE

ILINKA SQUARE

POKROVSKY BOULEVARD

WALK 2

AEET

RED SQUARE

ILINKA

KREMLIN

WALK 1

VARVARKA

STARAYA SQUARE

SOLYANKA STREET

YAUZSKY

KREMLIN EMBANKMENT

MOSKVORETSKAYA EMBANKMENT

MOSKVORETSKY BRIDGE

MOSKVORETSKAYA EMBANKMEN

Yauza River

ZAMOSKVARECHIYE

GREAT STONE BRIDGE

BOLSHAYA ORDYNKA

PYATNITSKAYA STREET

DMITROVA STREET

BOLSHAYA POLYANKA STREET

AL STREET

WALKS AND MAIN SIGHTS

Moscow

Walk 1: The Kremlin: A Tour of Its Ancient Buildings
Walk 2: Red Square and Kitai Gorod
Walk 3: Novodyevichi Convent
Walk 4: From the Arbat to Kachalova Street:
A View of Literary Moscow

0   Miles   1

0   Kilometers   1

Walk · 1

The Kremlin

A TOUR OF
ITS ANCIENT
BUILDINGS

The Cathedral of the Annunciation

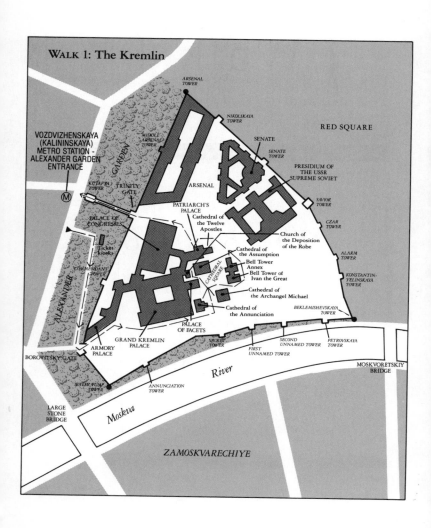

WALK 1: The Kremlin

VOZDVIZHENSKAYA
(KALININSKAYA)
METRO STATION -
ALEXANDER GARDEN
ENTRANCE

ARSENAL TOWER

NIKOLSKAYA TOWER

MIDDLE ARSENAL TOWER

SENATE

SENATE TOWER

RED SQUARE

PRESIDIUM OF THE USSR SUPREME SOVIET

GARDEN

KUTAFYA TOWER

TRINITY GATE

ARSENAL

SAVIOR TOWER

CZAR TOWER

PALACE OF CONGRESSES

PATRIARCH'S PALACE

Cathedral of the Twelve Apostles

Church of the Deposition of the Robe

ALARM TOWER

Ticket kiosks

COMMANDANT TOWER

Cathedral of the Assumption

Bell Tower Annex

Bell Tower of Ivan the Great

KONSTANTIN-YELINSKAYA TOWER

ALEXANDER

CATHEDRAL SQUARE

Cathedral of the Archangel Michael

Cathedral of the Annunciation

BEKLEMISHEVSKAYA TOWER

PALACE OF FACETS

SECRET TOWER

SECOND UNNAMED TOWER

PETROVSKAYA TOWER

BOROVITSKY GATE

GRAND KREMLIN PALACE

ARMORY PALACE

FIRST UNNAMED TOWER

River

MOSKVORETSKIY BRIDGE

WATER-PUMP TOWER

ANNUNCIATION TOWER

LARGE STONE BRIDGE

Moskva

ZAMOSKVARECHIYE

Starting Point: Kremlin, below the Kutafya Gate, at the entrance to the Alexander Garden (Aleksandrinsky Sad)

Walk Length: 2^1/$_2$–3 hours

Metro Stop: Vozdvizhenskaya on the Blue Line (until recently named Kalininskaya). Take the entrance leading to the Alexander Garden (Aleksandrinsky Sad).

The Kremlin is closed on Thursday. All other days hours are from 10:00 A.M. until 6:00 P.M. Tickets to the must-see Armory and Diamond Fund are available only at the Intourist office at 3 Tverskaya (formerly Gorky) Street. The tickets required for entry into the cathedral museums are available in the Alexander Garden, as described below.

The walk is based on an entry through the Borovitskaya Tower into the Kremlin grounds. If this gate is closed, enter through the Trinity Gate (where the walk concludes) and simply follow the map backwards to the nearby starting point. Because the Kremlin's monuments are so close to one another, there is not a lot of walking involved in this excursion. However, the Kremlin's churches were so powerful as precedent that this is the best introduction to Russian architecture.

There are no places for the public to eat on the Kremlin grounds. Restrooms are available on Cathedral Square behind the Assumption Cathedral, as marked on the map.

Kremlin. The word, meaning "fortress," and the place both evoke the strangeness of Russia. Here is where we begin our pursuit of the country on foot. "The Kremlin declared . . ." we hear almost daily in the news, as if the fortress spoke, which in a sense it does. Its form was shaped by what transpired within it. It is a map to the Russian psyche, a hieroglyph to decipher. Secrets lie in stone buildings, frescoes, icons, a cannon, a bell, and, when the past has been destroyed, the tangibility of old names. The name of the Kremlin hill itself, **Borovitsky**, derives from the word for conifer forest, which over a thousand years ago thickly covered the area. This walk will guide you through the Kremlin's oldest buildings and, we hope, into the mentality of the country.

Traces of history lie not only in the existing buildings but in basements and church foundations that also served the earlier buildings. The Kremlin is a major archeological site, yielding evidence of settlement thousands of years ago by an Iron Age culture, the Dyakovian. Tiering down through time, archeologists have found on the Kremlin grounds the remains of a tiny wooden house without a chimney (smoke escaped out the front door); wooden beams reinforcing old defenses dating from before the Mongol invasions; and the foundation of a destroyed fourteenth-century church serving as base to the magnificently ornate Terem Palace (1635–36). Everything now visible replaced an earlier, less opulent version.

Many peoples long past have valued the Borovitsky Hill, which commands the Moskva River. Arab money dating from the seventh century has been found in nearby deposits, a sign of the river's link to world trade in ancient times. In fact, the first grand duke of Muscovy, Ivan I, moved his residence here (when the site was devoid of stone buildings) from the far more glamorous city of Vladimir in the 1320s to take advantage of better geography. It was a strategic decision reminiscent of Peter the Great's move of the capital to St. Petersburg nearly 400 years later. Ivan I's judgment proved sound. His dynasty went on to unify the fractured Russian lands from a site that was first mentioned in the chronicles in 1147, centuries after other cities had flowered.

The Kremlin's lively red brick walls and bastions that we see today were raised by Italian architects largely from the 1480s through the 1490s. As defenses they were state of the art. The new walls replaced an earlier white lime-stone fortress built in 1369, which in turn had taken the place of Ivan I's wooden walls and towers dating from 1339, themselves an expansion of stockades erected for centuries or even millennia.

This improvement in defenses was undertaken by one of the most capable politicians to occupy the Kremlin, Grand Duke Ivan III (reigned 1462–1505). He oversaw the rise of Muscovy to preeminence among the other Russian states, many of which he gobbled up. To rule his growing lands he reformed the Kremlin administration and included commoners in powerful posts, to the great annoyance of the senior boyars, the Russian nobility. His cunning and obese wife, Sophia Paleologue, helped organize the intensive building that went on during his reign. Not only fortress walls but most of the Kremlin cathedrals were reconstructed in a new, more Western style, using Italian architects.

In fact, Ivan III can be described as a daring and early "Westernizer," starting with his decision to marry Sophia, a Roman Catholic brought up under the protection of the Pope. She was a niece of the last emperor of Byzantium, but after the fall of Constantinople had fled to Italy where she converted to the Western faith. The negotiations leading up to her betrothal to Ivan III were bizarre. The Pope harbored the hope that with his royal bait he could tempt the grand duke of Muscovy into the Latin fold. His faithless intermediary told the Pope that the Muscovites had no objection to a Catholic consort, all the while telling the Muscovites that the Pope had no objections to Sophia's reconverting to Orthodoxy.

Princess Sophia herself settled the question by promptly

reconverting as soon as she reached Russian lands. Throughout her life she proved a shrewd tactician, "very ugly, intelligent and scheming," in the words of one observer. Her greatest victory came years later when she managed to replace the legal heir to the grand duchy (Ivan III's grandson by an earlier marriage) with her own son, Vasily III. He in turn would father Ivan the Terrible.

We begin our walk at the foot of the **Kutafya Tower** (circa 1516), the only preserved example of a bridge fortification attached to the Kremlin. This sort of platform jutting out from the main wall was common when the Kremlin was surrounded by moats. On this side of the Kremlin the "moat" was in fact a river (the Neglinnaya), which now courses underground to the Moskva through a pipe laid in 1821. Our walk through the **Alexander Garden** to the Borovitskaya Tower is more or less down the "middle" of the river, which lapped a narrow bank below the walls. Pause for a moment and try to visualize the entire Kremlin ringed by water. The bridge (formerly a drawbridge) from the Kutafya Tower leads to the **Trinity Tower** (Troitskaya Bashnya) built in 1495–99, one of the Kremlin's main entrances.

The steep bastion roofs are late seventeenth-century additions in the Moscow Baroque style. Note how well they integrate with the early Renaissance military solidity below. Gilded czarist eagles survived on the new towers until 1935–37, when they were removed and replaced by the red star beacons, illuminated by electrical power day and night.

From the base of the Kutafya Tower we walk diagonally to the right toward a group of kiosks. There, tickets to the Kremlin cathedrals are sold. Ask for *vsye bilyeti* (all tickets) and continue your stroll to the right toward the corner **Borovitskaya Tower Gate** entrance.

The brick fortress was raised as Muscovy emerged into preeminence among the warring Russian grand

duchies and city states. Under Ivan III one city after another fell into Moscow's clutches. Powerful Novgorod was
subjected by turning commoners against their boyar rulers in the city's assembly, where all free males had a vote.
Gradually assuming authority, Ivan managed to dissolve
the democratic assembly and execute or deport thousands of citizens, thus destroying any potential opposition. Novgorod's boyars were killed and dumped into
Moscow's ponds, where they are said to have fed the carp
destined for Ivan's table, while their wives and daughters
were sold to Mongol harems. Vengeance was above all
public, meant to deter the slightest thought of resistance.

Despite his successful expansionism, Ivan had concerns to keep him lying awake at night. For one, the
savage Mongols kept demanding the taxes his ancestors
had given in the past to prevent invasions. One of the
Asiatics' favorite tactics during sieges was to catapult the
heads of fallen defenders homeward over the walls. They
also had an insatiable appetite for Russian slaves, and
incessant raids into Ivan's lands depopulated whole
towns and regions. Slung into nets dangling from Mongol
saddles, the Russian captives were transported eastward.
On the long journey many of the weakest and least valuable were stabbed to death and dumped by the wayside.

"The old and infirm men," recorded Emperor Maxi-
milian's ambassador to Muscovy in the early 1500s, "who
will not fetch much at a sale are given to the Tartar youths
(much as hares are given to whelps by way of their first
lesson in hunting), either to be stoned, or to be thrown
into the sea, or to be killed by any sort of death they
might please." The Muscovite embassies in Tartaria spent
thousands of rubles a year buying Russians out of captiv-
ity. When they balked at demanded ransoms, far higher
than the normal prices for slaves, the Mongols were
known to torture the captives in front of the envoys.

On his western flank, Ivan was threatened by the
Catholic kingdom of Lithuania, which had long been a
rival of Muscovy's for dominance of the Russian lands.

Ivan's agents told him that Lithuania and the Mongols were discussing alliance, a combination that posed a serious threat. The Golden Horde (one of several Mongol kingdoms) attacked successively in 1460, 1465, 1472, and 1480, the latter two campaigns mounted in expectation of Lithuanian support which never came. The last invasion, when the Mongol and Russian armies faced each other across a river without joining combat, is considered the date of the "Fall of the Tartar Yoke."

Muscovy's star may have been in the ascendant, but clearly the massive Kremlin battlements were warranted as insurance against a shift in fortune. Ivan III was unlikely to forget that his father, Vasily II, had been captured by the Mongols as recently as 1445, and released only with the payment of a massive ransom. And this mighty new citadel would indeed fall, though not under Ivan III's reign: to the Tartars in 1571, the Poles in 1610, and Napoleon in 1812.

The placid beauty of the Alexander Garden today is an irony of history. The shouts of commerce and bloodshed long ago echoed over the river that is now buried in a pipe below this park. We can imagine men, their heads full with plotting, gazing thoughtfully at the water. That element at least has not changed. The Kremlin is still the political center of the Soviet Union. Here Gorbachev has offices; here the Supreme Soviet and Council of Ministers meet. As we enter the Kremlin proper, many of the gray-suited men (and the occasional woman) you'll see are brooding over the same questions that consumed their boyar predecessors. What to do about Lithuania? How to handle the Moslem (Mongol) threat? How to keep Catholic Western Ukraine under Muscovite control?

We enter the Kremlin the back way, through a gate the grand dukes and czars used when they wanted their comings and goings to be unnoticed. The **Borovitskaya Tower Gate**, built in 1490, is up a rather steep hill to the left. Like the Trinity Tower Gate we saw at the beginning of the walk, it also housed a drawbridge crossing

Pathway through the Alexander Garden to the Borovitskaya Tower Gate

the Neglinnaya River, down whose "middle" we have just walked.

Through the gate immediately on the left is the **Armory Palace** (which also houses the Diamond Fund). The palace was built on the site of old stables in 1844–51, as a museum to house Kremlin treasures. The columns framing the second-story windows are carved in imitation of medieval folk and religious floral patterns. The **Grand Kremlin Palace** (1838–50), which begins adjacent and sprawls over a huge area encompassing many older buildings, has similar decoration. This is an attempt to keep the nineteenth-century construction consistent with the medieval sense of the Kremlin as a whole.

Look to your right as you walk: beyond the battlements, across the Moskva River, is the part of the city called **Zamoskvarechiye** (literally, beyond the Moskva River). The area was long ago settled by *streltsy* (shooters), the Kremlin's Praetorian Guard, as well as merchants who traded with the Golden Horde. One of the main avenues is still named the Ordynka—as the road taken to the "Orda," or Horde. Note how little is visible, from inside the fortress, of the Kremlin walls and towers. You are at the top of a hill, with the defenses built on the slope and screened by trees. This is what makes the Kremlin so lovely from a distance, with palaces and gilded churches rising high above the red brick battlements.

Moscow's center is **Cathedral Square**, which opens on your left at the end of the Grand Kremlin Palace. Here stand the most important cathedrals in Russia. They were all raised during the reign of Ivan III, with the exception of the Cathedral of the Archangel Michael. Even so, they have very different features. This is because the design provoked savage political fights, and the styles often changed. We can read the cathedrals on the square as a record of intrigue.

Ivan III must have been a very practical man. He entrusted the construction of Russia's most important church, the **Cathedral of the Assumption** (1475–79), directly across the square from where we have entered, to a foreigner, Aristotle Fioravanti of Italy. Here, Russia's metropolitans and later patriarchs (the leaders of the Russian Church) were buried, ceremonies of vassalage took place, and later the czars were crowned. To understand the daring of this move, one must realize that architectural features were determined by canon. To deviate was to commit heresy, and yet the grand duke commissioned a Roman Catholic, whose religion was anathema. Imagine, for example, President Eisenhower trying to rebuild the White House with the aid of a communist architect.

It is safe to see here the influence of the cosmopolitan Sophia, who had been brought up in Italy. Cultured, luxury-loving, fat, and crafty, she protected the invaluable Western specialists who were serving the Muscovite state. But there was only so much she could do, since these alien influences were terrifying to the conservative religious hierarchy.

Ivan III got additional help from God in this instance. An earlier Assumption Cathedral (1326–27), the first stone church in Moscow, had occupied the site but in old age required wooden posts for support. Two Russian architects dismantled the venerable church and began a new one. Once it had been built up to the vaults, a mild earthquake struck and the building collapsed. This placed the clergy, who had backed the original rebuilding, in a rather awkward position. Ivan III ascertained that the fault lay in the engineering and sent off to Italy for new designers.

Fioravanti answered the summons. He was sent first to study the Vladimir Cathedral of the Assumption (1158–89), regarded as the crown of Russian architecture, which was to serve as the model for the new church. It was important to emphasize the symbolic line of succession through the old capital of Vladimir back to the even more ancient center of Kiev. Fioravanti was building a potent symbol of Russia's unity under Moscow, and he labored under the scrutiny of many eyes. All of his plans had to meet the approval of the Orthodox Church.

In outward appearance the five-domed Kremlin Cathedral of the Assumption is very like the Vladimir model. It has similar proportions and wide, lovely arches above the same facade pilasters. These arches are known as *zakomari*. They delineate on the outside facade the course of interior vaults.

When a *zakomar* is pointed at the top (like a Gothic arch), it is known as a *kokoshnik*, or "woman's head-dress." In medieval Russia women wore pointed head-dresses, and architects borrowed the term to describe their pointed arches. Both *zakomari* and *kokoshniki* came to be used as purely decorative motifs, without regard to interior vaulting, and many churches combine both for lovely rhythmic effect. Such play is one of the most typical features of Russian architecture.

The Cathedral of the Assumption is decorated only by zakomari, as was consistent with the Vladimir precedent. Fioravanti did his work faithfully. But there is a subtle and profound difference for which he cannot be blamed. Look at the arcade relief banding the south wall facing the square. The relief columns have very simple orders, and at the bottoms are uncarved pedestals that simply slant back into the facade. By contrast, the Vladimir arcade columns have beautifully carved leafy capitals, and pedestals with some of the most extraordinary stone portraiture in Russia. In twelfth-century Vladimir, a flat stone facade flowered. The church's energy radiated from inside out to shape the facade.

In fifteenth-century Moscow, the same facade was a place to stick semi-classical decoration. That said, the Kremlin cathedral is noble in proportion and its eclecticism ingenuous, as if it adopted facade decoration because that was expected, like wearing a necktie. The dignified upsweep of its arches and golden cupolas could sustain anything the architect cared to attach.

While we are on the subject of facades, look directly across the square at the **Cathedral of the Archangel Michael** (1505–08), which is to the right of where we entered. Its Italian architect, Alevisio Novi, was also sent to Vladimir. The building exterior is divided into the same pilasters topped by the wide elegant *zakomari* of tradition, yet with an incredible addition: within the arches lie huge Venetian-style scallop shells. It is a wonderfully outrageous building, originally painted red and white. It is touching that Russian craftsmen adopted the foreign scallop as one of their favorite ornamental motifs. You will find it everywhere in later centuries, above doorways and windows and in moldings, silver work, and furniture.

Now look at the **Cathedral of the Annunciation** which is to the left of where we entered Cathedral Square (with our backs to the battlements and river). Its facade makes a completely different impression. *Kokoshniki* surge up from the walls like waves to crash toward the golden cupolas. Notice how much more dynamic they are than the rounded *zakomari* that are just below the cupolas and mark the windows and the entrances to the cathedral. The counterpoint is subtle and effective. The facade of the church seems to ripple like water stirred by wind. In scale, decorative brickwork, and use of *kokoshniki*, the Cathedral of the Annunciation is a highly traditional building.

The churches on Cathedral Square have very different facades. Yet none of this variety alters the similarity of all the church interiors. Inside each, a fresco-covered chamber leads to a towering barrier of icons, the iconostasis, which shields the altar from the nave. There is a disjunction between church exteriors, which absorb a multitude of influences, and the interiors, which mirror the unchanging liturgy. This is a perfect metaphor for Russian culture, outwardly absorbing influences from every quarter yet keeping a secret essence intact. Only after eighty years would St. Basil's Cathedral on nearby Red Square (Walk 2) manage to externalize the secrets of the iconostasis into stone and brick. The result was a mysterious and utterly original work, one of the greatest buildings in the world.

Now, walk back across the square to step inside the **Cathedral of the Assumption**. Much of Muscovy's ceremonial life was centered inside the spacious house of worship. Here Ivan the Terrible crowned himself czar (a word derived from "Caesar") in 1547, the first Muscovite leader officially to claim the title. His carved wooden throne stands toward the altar on the right. In a way, the light-filled interior is an anomaly, unlike the dimness of earlier churches. Fioravanti also kept the interior more open than usual, and even the supporting columns do little to block lines of vision around the church. Taken as a hole, this church is more radical than the outwardly daring Archangel Cathedral (with its scallop shells), which more closely retains the interior shape of old.

All the same, Orthodoxy overcame the building's innovative openness: fresco overwhelms the interior space, and the massive gilt iconostasis is the undeniable focus of attention. The original frescoes and iconostasis were painted by the great Dionysius in 1481–1515. Some of this work is visible in sections where the iconostasis has been opened, revealing walls that were covered up before the cathedral was repainted. The rest of the cathedral's fresco was redone in 1642–43 by 150 artists gathered from almost every major Russian city, who largely followed the earlier plan. Restoration preserves this seventeenth-century fresco, and in some places even reveals more of Dionysius's original work. A schematic explanation of the frescoes is available in English on plaques.

The most precious relic in any Russian city was an icon representing its patron saint, and with each conquest Muscovy appropriated this image (and others) for the Assumption Cathedral. Moscow thus absorbed greater and greater spiritual protection, and diminished the power of its erstwhile enemies. This policy of spiritual growth by military conquest makes the cathedral one of the best places to study icons because of the range of styles and centuries represented.

Southern portal to the Cathedral of the Assumption

The wide-open cathedral is like a jewelbox holding these treasures. The fact of an Italian designer symbolizes Muscovy's ascent from one duchy among many to European power, conscious of international culture. Moscow had its own earlier architectural tradition, largely destroyed or replaced by later churches, but its greatest work emerged after this period of considered eclecticism.

The churches on Cathedral Square represent a middle phase in the evolution of Muscovite style. They are an exultant display of a young state's newfound power and religious fervor, and served as models to innumerable later churches around the grand duchy. It was not only the buildings themselves that were copied but the layout of Cathedral Square, with churches and a belltower hemming in an open area. Whatever transpired here at the center established precedent.

Take a few minutes to stroll around the square. Foreign ambassadors were received by the grand dukes and czars in the **Palace of Facets** (1487–91), the strange building jutting into the square between the Cathedrals of the Assumption and the Annunciation. It was built by Italians Marco Friazin and Pietro Antonio Solari (designer of most of the Kremlin bastions). The hall received its name from the diamond-shaped carving on the wall facing the square, with red patterns painted on the brick side walls. Those fabulous windowframes are a product of the late seventeenth century, whose architecture we will see more of on the second walk. Unfortunately, the Palace of Facets is not open to the public, since it is still used for state occasions (along with the Hall of St. George in the Grand Kremlin Palace). Watch your television carefully the next time there is a summit in Moscow. Every inch of the wide, vaulted space is covered by fresco, stone, or wood carving. After such abundance the terse exterior is like a wall of hard diamonds.

Imagine the square's activity in centuries past, with carriages clattering arrival, clocktowers chiming, the

The facade of the Palace of Facets

shouted sounds of trade drifting from a distance, and boyars crisscrossing in fancy dress. "His upper garment is of cloth of golde, silke or cloth, long, down to the foote, and buttened with great buttons of silver, or els laces of silke," described a sixteenth-century English ambassador of the Russian aristocracy.

Suddenly, rounding the Belltower of Ivan the Great, two *streltsy* drag a man, dressed in rags but well spoken, onto the square: "Let go of me, you swine," he screams. "I have a wife and children to feed!"

"It is the will of the Czar!" a *strelets* answers. "Shut

up or we'll arrest you." With that they drag him into the Cathedral of the Annunciation. No one on the square shows the slightest interest in the altercation. Another painter is being dragged to work. The creators of the frescoes and icons we now enjoy were often impressed craftsmen, wretchedly underpaid. They tried to escape the Kremlin commissions, to return to the regional cities from which they had been rousted. It was far more profitable to work for private patrons than to be placed "on salary" in the Moscow Kremlin, and the archives are full of petitions from painters begging for additional money to pay for lodgings, or to avoid starvation.

Let's follow our painter into the **Cathedral of the Annunciation** (1484–89), whose cascading roofline we have already noticed. Even though it was built shortly after the Assumption Cathedral, it radiates a different power. It was designed in traditional style by Pskov architects who had worked with Fioravanti. The cathedral was the private chapel of the grand dukes and czars, and far from being a symbol of empire, served as a warning to them. Its frescoes include passages illustrating the Book of Revelation, with the torments described on the cathedral walls (for example, above the arches facing the iconostasis) designed to give pause to the most ruthless potentate.

These frescoes refer to contemporary politics. Starting in the reign of Ivan III, the Orthodox Church was riven by a furious dispute over its lands and wealth, very similar to what was then happening in the West as the Reformation began. Church liberals and mystics wanted to divest property, give alms to the poor, concentrate on prayer, and avoid politics. They were strongly supported by the grand duke, who cast a covetous eye on church lands. But this liberal faction lost, and lost badly. Church conservatives were able to smear them with the accusation of heresy, and the frescoes (1508; repainted 1547) picture their punishment as well as warn secular rulers. These disputes erupted first under Ivan III, and then anew during the reigns of Vasily III and Ivan the Terrible.

Let's imagine our ragged painter again, this time working intently on a scaffold inside the cathedral. The year is 1547, and he is repainting frescoes damaged by the fire that greeted Ivan the Terrible's rise to power. He paints over the drying plaster, and ignores the sound of footsteps below. Silence, broken only by the faint rasp of his brush, reigns. Then the footsteps leave. "It was probably Bishop Sylvester," he thinks to himself, looking down. "But why did he say nothing?" He pauses in his painting of Chastity, and then works anew, giving her the features of his beloved Anna. Next to her on the Gates of Heaven stand Reason (his best friend, Pavel), Purity (his daughter, Natasha) and Right (Bishop Sylvester). He chuckles to himself, already visualizing the Gates of Hell.

A nasty fight was brewing. The footsteps belonged not to the relatively liberal Bishop Sylvester but to a senior *dyak* named Viskovaty. The more Viskovaty looked at the painting, the more sure he was. They were heretical! Latin figures stood on the gates of Heaven and Hell; Air was as a maiden; Time was winged with the four seasons. There was no precedent for this. At a church council in 1553, he accused Sylvester of heresy, pointing to the frescoes and to his friendship with a convicted freethinker named Bashkin. Some of the offending allegorical frescoes were repainted, but Viskovaty had pressed his luck too hard.

"You started with a crusade against the heretics," the powerful Metropolitan Makary snapped at him during Sylvester's trial, "and now you turn to pseudo-philosophizing about the icons. Take care not to be caught as a heretic yourself." The metropolitan was no liberal, but he liked the new art. He even went so far as to defend unusual, naturalistic details in icons at a church council in 1554. Thus, even as the religious conservatives consolidated power, they allowed new Italianate themes to enter painting.

The cathedral's iconostasis is the oldest complete example preserved today, and includes icons dating back to the late fourteenth century. Three of Russia's greatest painters are represented here: Theophanes the Greek is credited with the tall, silhouetted images spanning the third row from the bottom; the fourth row is divided between Andrei Rublev for the icons on the left (with the exception of the fourth), and Prokhor of Gorodets for the icons on the right.

An entire cosmos of saints and angels, the true rulers of the earth, constitutes the iconostasis. The stakes of the religious disputes become clear: the order of the invisible world was being determined. All gestures of creation were suffused with religious meaning, hence any innovation was attempted at the risk of one's soul.

Keeping the dangers of innovation in mind, our next destination will come as a relief. We are yet again going to cross the square. To the west of the Assumption Cathedral is the diminutive **Church of the Deposition of the Robe** (1484–86), built as the private chapel of the metropolitan. The single-cupola church gives an idea of what early Muscovite architecture looked like, especially when you visualize it freestanding without the covered galleries to north and west. It originally had the open porch you see to the south on those two sides. When you compare it with the looming Assumption Cathedral adjacent, you begin to understand what a shock Fiora-vanti's creation must have been. It is important to emphasize that the shifts in style from one church to another were not accidental. Both the Cathedral of the Annunciation and the Church of the Deposition can be read as clerical reaction to Ivan III's import of foreigners, as well as to his dabbling in "heretical" doctrines.

Inside (where there are also exhibits of religious folk art), compare the seventeenth-century iconostasis of Nazary Istomin with the fourteenth- and fifteenth-century icons in the Annunciation Cathedral. The older paintings have a brooding depth that the later ones lack. Istomin's icons are marked by emblems of rank and a lovely curvilinear sameness, a hint of the formulaic. Spirituality remains, but it is channeled through style rather than discovered freshly. Istomin had the good fortune of patronage from the boyar-merchant Stroganov family, which has given its name to an entire seventeenth-century school of icon painting. Its ornate eloquence is poverty of another sort, beside the deeply expressive icons of earlier days.

After exiting from the church, look above and behind it. The eleven cupolas with colorful tilework on the supporting drums were built in 1681, as a golden crown to several separate chapels. The chapels are hidden away inside the **Terem Palace** (1635–37), which is not open to the public. It is hard not to suspect Islamic influence in the minaretlike array of Terem towers.

Another hint of the Moslem East may lie in the calligraphic scroll unwinding near the top of the **Belltower of Ivan the Great** across the square. The lower tiers of the belltower were built in 1505–08 by Italian Bon Friazin, with the last tier and a half (including calligraphy) added by Czar Boris Godunov in 1600. The script simply explains that the tower was finished and gilded in the second year of Tsar Boris's reign. The tower's bells, the largest of which could be heard for thirty kilometers, are unlikely ever to ring again. Napoleon ordered the tower destroyed as he began his retreat from Moscow, and while explosives did not bring it down, the foundation is so damaged that such ringing could cause a collapse.

The annex housing additional bells that is adjacent to the tower was built in 1632. Inside is the **Museum of Applied Art** with exhibits of vestments, jewelry, liturgical items, and decorative objects produced in the Kremlin studios.

Belltowers played a very important role in Russian architecture, and not simply to peal parishoners to service. They naturally had to break the cubic form of other churches and thus offered architects a vision of pure height. When the great "tent"-style churches emerged later in the sixteenth century, of which St. Basil's Cathedral is the preeminent example, belltowers were one of the sources.

The **Cathedral of the Archangel Michael**, whose

The Belltower of Ivan the Great and the adjoining annex

scallop-shell facade arches we have already noticed, is our next destination. It was built at the same time as the belltower, in 1505–08, in the very first years of Vasily III's reign. He followed his parents' radical building programs, but as we noted before, this cathedral's daring is only skin-deep. Once we enter we are again in Old Russia. The cathedral became the burial site of Moscow's grand dukes and czars, from Ivan I (who moved his residence from Vladimir, thus starting Moscow on its upward road to power) to Peter the Great's predecessor, Fyodor III. Peter himself established a new resting place for the czars in the Cathedral of Peter and Paul in St. Petersburg.

Behind the iconostasis lies the holiest ground of the church, the burial place of saints. It is here that Ivan the Terrible had buried first the son he had murdered in a rage, and then himself. This part of the cathedral is closed to the public, which is doubly unfortunate because only here is the original sixteenth-century fresco intact. The walls above the casket embody the mad czar's program: assault on the boyars. The story of Lazarus is illustrated to underline the guilt of the wealthy before the poor, and on the eastern wall an enigmatic scene shows a man about to be arrow-shot during a feast, perhaps a dishonest boyar being brought down by an Angel of Death.

The frescoes in the main body of the cathedral date from 1652–66, but were careful copies of the older work. Yakov Kazanets, Stepan Rezanets, Sidor Pospeev, Simon Ushakov, and other painters participated in the repainting, including passages devoted to the exploits of Archangel Michael, the patron saint of Russia's warriors. On the northern wall he destroys the Assyrian horde before Gideon and his army.

A late fourteenth-century icon in the iconostasis of winged Michael in a red robe is said to have been commissioned by the wife of Dmitri Donskoy in celebration of his 1378 victory at Kulikova, the first defeat the Muscovites inflicted on the Tartars. Nothing better illustrates

The Czar's Pushka *and one-ton cannonballs*

the link between history and religion in the Russian imagination, a conception common, of course, to other people. The Bible was the best textbook of history, its archetypal patterns redrawn as God worked his will in the world. Painting was both prayer and propaganda. The brush offered fabulous power: honored ancestors were placed alongside saints and angels, as if they were participants in the same titanic spiritual struggle.

Pass again outdoors and walk around the Belltower of Ivan the Great to the side opposite the square. A rather surreal sight awaits. Mounted on a pedestal is the **Czar Bell**, the largest in the world, weighing 200 tons and cast in 1737. When the metal had been heated to a glowing red, a fire broke out in the Kremlin, and the water used by firefighters reached the casting pit and caused the bell to crack. There it lay for 100 years until it was dug up and placed on display.

This all makes sense, even if it is a disappointment to lovers of carillon. But then we notice another swollen effort at casting a few yards to the north, the **Czar Cannon**, cast in 1586. Two such toys on a scale for giants can hardly be a coincidence. The cannonballs weigh one ton each! This magnificently useless gun was cast as Russia hurtled toward the Time of Troubles, with pretenders to the throne, civil war, and foreign occupation soon to come. The cannon is a wistful invocation to Mars, an image of the power Russia would have liked to wield as it approached collapse. It is a child's fantasy of limitless strength, so divorced from reality that it charms rather than frightens. The Czar's *Pushka* (cannon) is symbolic, an accidental work of art rather than a weapon, in which intent to harm gets hopelessly confused with the imagination.

And what of the bell the pious would have used to ring the call to prayer? It is hard to imagine 200 tons of tone. The metallic waves would have shaken the soul if it can indeed be reached by bell ringing. The bizarre ambition that animated the casting of the cannon is somehow more appropriate here as religious passion. In their own way the bell and the cannon are as eloquent about Russia as the most sublime cathedral.

The last building we visit on this walk is the **Patriarch's Palace**. As you walk around the building (the entrance is on the opposite side from the square), you get a good view of its private **Cathedral of the Twelve Apostles** (1643–46). Notice the resemblance to the Assumption Cathedral built 160 years earlier, with five gilded cupolas above slit windows, rounded *zakomar* arches, and the triple apse.

Its builder, Patriarch Nikon, was offended by the non-canonical church architecture that had developed in the sixteenth century (of which there are no examples on Cathedral Square), and his domestic cathedral is a clear expression of his program, which forced Muscovite architecture to return to old models. In 1655 he managed to outlaw the new "tent"-style churches, thus ending Russia's most original contribution to world architecture.

Yet Nikon was not conservative in everything. He reformed the liturgy to correct errors in the translations of old Greek texts, thus bringing on a schism that has never healed. The Old Believers refused to accept these changes and, facing persecution, fled as far as Siberia to worship as they pleased. Not only did they preserve the traditional liturgy but also old styles of dress, painting, and wooden architecture.

Enter first the main vaulted hall on your right as you come up the steps to the second floor. Huge ovens for the preparation of chrism (holy oil), then made only in the Kremlin once every two or three years, now dominate the chamber. Fifty aromatic ingredients went into the oil, which was used in coronations, the sanctification of churches, and on the baptismal robes of infants. After 1763 the ovens were moved here and the hall, which had been used for church congresses and to receive ambassadors, became known as the **Chrism Chamber**. Along the walls are cases displaying liturgical art and implements.

To the left (as you come up the stairs), and through an enfilade of rooms, lies the **Cathedral of the Twelve Apostles**. On the way make sure to look out the windows, which have a wonderful view of Cathedral Square. The iconostasis is not original but its icons represent the seventeenth century very well. Look at the dense realism in their backgrounds. The same spirit of investigation that led to reform of church texts brought about this naturalism, which was the death knell of mysticism. The Old Believers preserved traditional-style painting, and there were other conservatives in the church that sharply criticized the new work. In a way they were right, but the tide of the modern age was creeping up, soon to become a flood with Peter the Great's reforms.

Western motifs and ideas had always been a presence in Russian culture, but until late in the seventeenth century these imports were adapted to Russian ends. The icons here reveal the undigested influence of the West. Russia's creative essence was proving less able to absorb the new and maintain its integrity at the same time.

Much of the fault lies with the church hierarchy,

which was hostile to the spontaneous inventions of Russian artists. By stifling them, the church weakened Russia's antibodies to the onslaught of foreign culture. Clerics wanted to fix iconography and architecture strictly according to Byzantine and Old Russian precedents, a desire poisonous to true art. The ban on "tent"-style churches is a perfect example, and painters fared no better. "The higher circles," bitterly wrote art historian Nikodim Kondakov in exile in Prague in the 1920s, "made the worst possible use of an artistic craft which had succeeded in growing up upon Russian soil, depriving it even of liberty in its activity and reducing to nothing its achievements and material prosperity. One might really think that in the matter of State exploitation of the common stock of spiritual forces the Moscow offices were the precursors of the Bolsheviks."

The Soviet Union today seems to be fighting the same battles that have plagued it throughout history, and the Kremlin remains a silent, absorbing witness. Today's Patriarch Alexei has made clear his preference for stern measures that will hold the empire together.

At this point, exit the residence of his predecessors. Diagonally to the right, across an asphalt plaza, are two more recent buildings in which political dramas are now unfolding. One flattened corner of the triangular **Senate Building** (1776–87) by Matvei Kazakov is visible to us from here. (It is yellow with white detailing and a green roof.) Catherine the Great had it built in spare classical style to house the Senate she reorganized with administrative reforms of the 1760s. Quickly enough she determined that autocracy was the only effective means of ruling Russia; in a famous correspondence with Voltaire, her professed desire to establish a monarchy in line with the values of the *philosophes* proved to be propaganda. The building now houses offices of the Council of Ministers, and the Museum of Lenin's Apartment, where the founder of the Soviet State lived and worked from 1918 to 1923.

Adjacent on the right is the **Presidium of the USSR Supreme Soviet**, an innocuous structure that was built in 1932–34 to harmonize with the Senate. Behind the bland facade the fate of the Soviet Union is being decided in parliamentary debates. It is the Supreme Soviet that selects the president of the country for a five-year term and determines what powers will be legally granted to the executive. It remains an open question whether liberals will succeed in changing the country into a true democracy, but if they do much of the battle will have been fought within the walls of the Kremlin.

The **Savior Tower** (Spasskaya Bashnya), which serves as the Kremlin's main ceremonial gate, rises above the Presidium to the right. It is easy to pick out because of the huge clock face mounted on the tower and the sound of chimes that mark the quarter-hour. The very first clock was installed in 1625 by an Englishman named Christopher Galloway, although it was replaced long ago.

The **Trinity Gate** by which we will exit the Kremlin is only a short walk from the patriarch's residence. With your back to the residence, turn to the left. The gateway will appear very shortly, beyond the ultramodern **Palace of Congresses** (1961) by M. Posokhin, a well-designed building (reminiscent of Eero Saarinen's CBS Headquarters in New York) in an inappropriate setting.

Directly across the street from the Palace of Congresses is the **Arsenal** (1702–36), built on orders of Peter the Great from his basic design. It is easily recognizable from the cannon that line the facade, some of which were cast inside, others were captured from the French during the Napoleonic Wars. This building also suffered greatly during the French occupation of Moscow in 1812. Napoleon ordered that it be blown up along with many other Kremlin monuments (but not before he had stripped them of their gold and silver).

The Kremlin's bastions are a measure of the threat enemies have posed. When Russians have lost wars, or even had temporary setbacks, it has been at terrible cost.

Walk through the Trinity Gate and onto the ramp that leads to the outer **Kutafya Tower Gate**, where we began this walk. From the parapeted ramp (which once crossed a moat) you get an intimidating view of the walls.

Across the street from the Kutafya Gate is the old **Manege**, and off to the right the **Manege Square**, which recently had its name changed back from the Fiftieth Anniversary of October Square. It is here that mass demonstrations against the government have been unfolding, with tens—and sometimes hundreds—of thousands of citizens chanting in unison, "Retire!" The Kremlin walls undoubtedly give the Soviet leadership a sense of security in such times, and it remains to be seen whether they will once again prove their utility.

Walk · 2

Red Square and Kitai Gorod

Window of the abbot's residence

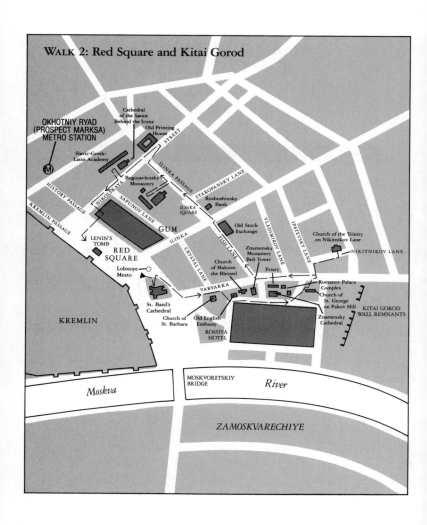

WALK 2: Red Square and Kitai Gorod

OKHOTNIY RYAD
(PROSPECT MARKSA)
METRO STATION

Cathedral
of the Savior
Behind the Icons

Old Printing
House

STREET

Slavic-Greek-
Latin Academy

NIKOLSKAYA

ILINKA PASSAGE

STAROPANSKY LANE

HISTORY PASSAGE

Bogoyavlensky
Monastery

SAPUNOV LANE

Ryabushinsky
Bank

KREMLIN PASSAGE

ILINKA
SQUARE

Old Stock
Exchange

GUM

ILINKA

FISH LANE

VLADIMIROV LANE

IPATEVSKY LANE

Church of the Trinity
on Nikitnikov Lane

LENIN'S
TOMB

Znamensky
Monastery
Bell Tower

NIKITNIKOV LANE

RED
SQUARE

CRYSTAL LANE

Church of
Maksim
the Blessed

Friary

Romanov Palace
Complex

Lobnoye
Mesto

VARVARKA

Church of
St. George
on Pskov Hill

KITAI GOROD
WALL REMNANTS

St. Basil's
Cathedral

Church of
St. Barbara

Old English
Embassy

ROSSIYA
HOTEL

Znamensky
Cathedral

KREMLIN

MOSKVORETSKIY
BRIDGE

River

Moskva

ZAMOSKVARECHIYE

Starting Point: Red Square, near St. Basil's Cathedral
Walk Length: 3 hours
Metro Stop: Okhotniy Ryad (Hunter Row) on the Red Line (until recently named Prospect Marksa). Take the underpass from the metro that leads to the corner of Istorichesky Proezd (History Passage) at the northern end of Red Square. As you come up the stairs, Red Square will be visible straight ahead of you.

This is a long walk so be prepared for exercise. There are several restaurants nearby or along the route, as listed at the end of the book, for which you might want to make reservations. It is also possible to get a snack at the Rossiya Hotel without reservations, as described below.

There is also a Kitai Gorod metro stop, which we do not recommend because it is too far away from where the walk begins.

Below the spired eastern walls of the Kremlin, Red Square is an open space in which innumerable dramas have unfolded: riots, public executions, celebrations of great military victories, and, more recently, parades marking anniversaries of the Bolshevik Revolution. Its power as the public heart of Moscow is evidenced by a recent decree: the national government, not the liberal Moscow City Council, will provide permits for demonstrations on Red Square. The square is too symbolic, too close to the center of power, to be relinquished even after the democrats seized city government.

Old and new Russia coexist here. St. Basil's Cathedral (1552–61), fantastical with color and wild shapes, shares the plaza with the sleek, modern tomb (1924–30) of Bolshevism's embalmed saint, Lenin. This walk takes us through Moscow's oldest district (aside from the Kremlin itself), but concludes at Lenin's Tomb, where Russia's communist revolutionaries put their mark on the city's most historic square.

Centuries ago Red Square was built up with countless trading stalls, churches, and homes, almost all wooden. In 1493 a massive fire reduced everything to ash. Ivan III (who built most of the Kremlin as we now see it) ordered that a swath be left clear as a firebreak protecting the Kremlin. Thus Moscow's central plaza was born with the apt name of Fire Square. After St. Basil's Cathedral was built, the square became known as *Krasnaya*, which then meant "beautiful." *Krasnaya* now means "red," hence the current name, which has nothing to do with the events of 1917.

Farther to the east stretches Kitai Gorod (China Town), the oldest quarter of Moscow outside of the Kremlin. Before Ivan III's order to leave clear the firebreak, houses crept right up to the Kremlin wall. Thus, Red Square is an integral part of Kitai Gorod, and was even carved out of it. Strangely, the name has nothing to do with China (*Kitai* means "China" in Russian), but derives from the old word *kita*, for earth-filled baskets which were used to reinforce wooden ramparts. Kitai Gorod today preserves churches and boyar palaces of the seventeenth century as well as Moscow's commercial district of the nineteenth century.

We begin the walk near St. Basil's Cathedral at the raised, circular platform with steps, **Lobnoye Mesto** (Protruding Place), where the head of the Biblical Adam was said to be buried. Here the czars' edicts were read to the public, including orders for execution, in which case the gallows waited alongside. When it was reconstructed in its current form in 1786, it had already long served as megaphone to the city.

One of the most romantic characters to meet the executioner here was the Cossack leader Stenka Razin, who led an uprising that nearly toppled the czar in 1670–71. Razin's revolt was powered by peasant fury at the strengthening bonds of serfdom, which had been instituted beginning only late in the fifteenth century. Some Russian serfs knew that their ancestors had once been free, and they periodically erupted into bloodthirsty rampages against officials and gentry landowners. Most often these outbreaks were local in scale, concerned with revenge against brutal overseers, rape of gentry daughters, and the looting and burning of the Big Houses overlooking vast estates. Occasionally the incendiary rage spread over entire provinces, the heat forming leaders and an inchoate agenda for liberty.

Razin guided a revolt that at its peak controlled almost the entire course of the Volga to the Caspian Sea, as well as the Donets and Don rivers, an area about 1,200 miles east to west and 1,500 miles north to south. Imagine John Brown's stand at Harper's Ferry spreading to cover most of the southern states, and you get an idea of the scale of Razin's achievement, as well as the terror he provoked in the czar. After many reverses, czarist troops finally began to gain and Razin was served up by his own associates.

"The streets teemed with spectators, some coming out of their houses to watch the extraordinary spectacle, others moved to indignation or even pity," a contemporary described his parade to execution on Red Square. "All his body was a living sore, so that the knout fell on raw bones. He was stubbornly brave, never uttered a cry or a whimper and only reproached his brother (tortured as appallingly) for 'his lack of courage.' "

During Razin's war many captured prisoners were kept in Savior Tower (Spasskaya Bashnya), the tall, star-topped bastion with the clock that is the main gate to the Kremlin. It was built by Pietro Solari in 1491, with the "tent" roof added in the seventeenth century. In front of this tower later was dug a wide moat, which connected the Moskva and Neglinnaya rivers, and completed sur-rounding the three-sided Kremlin with water. On each side of the moat lay an additional low wall with parapets. Add to this the sometimes audible screams of prisoners being tortured in the chambers of the **Konstantin-Yelininskaya Tower** (third to the left of the Savior Tower), and it is safe to say that in old days the Kremlin made an even more formidable impression than it does today.

Yet protest also took forms other than violence. We now turn our attention to **St. Basil's Cathedral**, just be-low the Lobnoye Mesto. The cathedral is a rare example in architecture of a building with psychological charge, and it seems to comment on Ivan the Terrible's reign. It is a perfect emblem of its age, a very good place to try to fathom sixteenth-century Russian culture.

The cathedral originally consisted of nine wooden chapels built to celebrate successive victories in Ivan the Terrible's historic campaign against the Tartars, peaking in his 1554 capture of Kazan. From 1555 to 1561 these churchlets were reconstructed in stone by architects Posnick and Barma, about whom very little is known. Officially named the Cathedral of the Interces-sion on the Moat, we now call the cathedral St. Basil's because in 1588 Basil the Blessed, an outspoken critic of Ivan the Terrible, was buried in the northeast chapel. Almost immediately afterward the monument to the czar's greatest victory came to celebrate his foremost adversary.

It is not merely in name that St. Basil's is subversive. It is the best of the famous "tent"-style churches that so angered the conservative clergy. Remember that religious architecture was the province of the church, and that Byzantine and Old Russian precedents were dictated by law. An instant in front of St. Basil's reveals how different it is from the correct boxlike churches of the Kremlin. The floor plan of St. Basil's is a crystal rather than a rectangle; its body is shattered into separate spires; and most important, its towering center is a *shatyor* (tent) narrowing to a tiny peak.

The cathedral draws on elements of older churches: *kokoshniki* and *zakomari* in the most complex combinations ever; cupolas, here twisted and wrought with wood-inspired patterns; and the arcaded base on which the ensemble of spires is mounted. But the overall effect is radical and spellbinding. From the time it was built, foreigners and Russians alike have been awed by its inexplicable beauty.

Russian architecture had broken formula and was speaking from the depths of the national psyche. The division between exterior and interior that we noted in the Kremlin churches (Walk 1) is rent. The facade fractures into a multitude of arrows and tiers, and seems to be saying something we cannot quite understand. Brutal with violent twists and spikes, outlandish color (added in the seventeenth century), and foliate abundance, it is sharp like the lash of a whip. The church is "read" by following the jagged, uneven routes upward to tortuous cupolas. This route is an image of the struggle of life. The entire arsenal of Russian decorative motifs is fired into a symbolic language.

Only one cupola (at the very top of the *shatyor*) is gilded, tiny like the eye of a needle. Golden domes, so prominent in older churches, are symbolic of heaven. The gilded eye here suggests that heaven is the reward of those who have traversed the torments that lie below, pictured in the church's twisting facade.

"If you are just and pious as you say, why did you fear a guiltless death, which is no death but gain?" This taunt of Ivan the Terrible's is as perfect as the cathedral. It was directed at Prince Kurbsky, once Ivan's bosom friend and foremost general, who had defected to Lithuania as the czar's paranoia reached maniacal proportions. A bitter fifteen-year correspondence between the two ensued. Ivan never tired of contrasting the courage of Kurbsky's servant, who delivered the first letter ("standing at death's door he did not hesitate to praise you in Our presence"), with the "cowardice" of the fled master. St. Basil's can be read as a monument to those like the servant who stayed and received the ultimate reward.

Equally an expression of the age were the *yurodiviye* (holy fools) who wandered often naked through the city streets, uttering prophecies and taking alms. Among them were charlatans and the demented, but also the truly spiritual. Current politics, the church hierarchy, and even the czar himself were denounced in allegory, and sometimes with daring openness. The cloak of immunity, granted by long custom, protected these penniless dissidents from the wrath of the powerful.

St. Basil is one of the most famous of these early objectors. As legend has it, his *yurodivy* qualities emerged during an apprenticeship as a bootmaker. Taking an order from a wealthy boyar for elaborate shoes, he burst out laughing and crying at the same time, for he saw that his client would die before the work was done. Later he began wandering the city naked and became known for discerning devils in daily life. Once he tore down an icon hanging above a city gate to reveal that the Virgin was painted over an image of Lucifer. By legend, he even fathomed the most popular beggar in Moscow, from whom the almsgiver received a heavenly bliss for the rest of his life, as an agent of the devil.

And he is said to have challenged the terrifying despot of Russia. During the pillage of Novgorod by Ivan's secret police (*Oprichniki*), Basil was living in the town in a cave under a bridge. He called Ivan to him and offered him meat to eat.

"I cannot eat meat," the czar answered, "I am a Christian and now is the Easter fast."

"Then why," asked Basil, "do you drink Christian blood?"

The renaming of the cathedral shows that the public sensed its true meaning as a picture of suffering leading to salvation. It is as much a comment on its age as are Solzhenitsyn's *Gulag Archipelago* and Shostakovich's Fourteenth Symphony. Russian architecture was finally absorbing the same expressiveness that had long filled icons. Angry complaints of the clergy that the forms were noncanonical led nowhere. From the moment it was completed, the cathedral became the most loved building in Moscow.

St. Basil's was a church into which townspeople did not go. With room for only a few worshipers, it was reserved for the royal family and its intimates. Take time now to enter the museum inside, open every day except Tuesdays from 9:30 A.M. to 5:30 P.M. (last entry at 5:00).

The diminutive interior chapels are going to surprise you after the grand expression of the exterior. The first chambers house a museum that charts the building of the monument, and weapons and artifacts from Ivan the Terrible's campaign against the Tartars. The original iconostases were destroyed during one of many fires, and the current altar barriers date from the late sixteenth and seventeenth centuries. In the vaults below, Basil is buried with the manacles he wore in perpetual penance.

On your way out, take note of the two large bronze figures with a sword and shield, mounted on a pedestal in front of the cathedral. The monument (1804–18) by Ivan Martos celebrates Prince Pozharsky and a commoner named Minin, who raised the forces that threw Polish occupiers out of Moscow in 1612. Russia had collapsed as the result of struggles over succession, and the Poles had seized the throne. The war effort organized by Pozharsky and Minin led to the establishment of the Romanov dynasty in 1613, which ruled on through to the 1917 Revolution.

We now head into Kitai Gorod proper, following a looping course that will bring us back into Red Square. Walk eastward down the **Varvarka** (Barbara Street),

Rooftops along the Varvarka

which recently had its traditional name restored from
Stenka Razin (the executed Cossack) Street. It was a prestige address, lined with foreign embassies and boyar
mansions. Down this road in 1378 Russian troops
marched to the field of Kulikova, where they won their
first victory ever over Tartar forces.

"From early morning to late at night is the incessant
sound of equipages," an 1833 Russian guidebook described. "You see cartloads of goods and you can't cross
from the number of carriages. . . . Here are Siberians, Little Russians, Poles, Tartars, French, Jews, Germans, English, Persians and Armenians, senior officials, the rich,
and the indigent."

A merchant made rich in this international milieu
paid for the yellow **Church of St. Barbara** (1796–
1804) by Rodion Kazakov, at #2 Varvarka on your right.
It is a typical and lovely example of Russian classicism.
St. Basil's on Red Square set a standard for beauty
through the end of the seventeenth century, but after Peter the Great founded St. Petersburg in 1703, Western

sources became paramount. The Church of St. Barbara, built 100 years later, shows how fully Russian architecture in that span of time had diverted itself into the Western mainstream.

Next, at #4 Varvarka, is the **Old English Embassy** (early sixteenth century), which Ivan the Terrible gave to English envoys as a residence starting in 1556. The embassy is best seen from the driveway in front of the Rossiya Hotel skyscraper. The deep eaves and tiny windows, which would have been filled with mica or translucent sheepskin, are typical of wealthy houses of the period. Originally a covered wooden stairway probably led diagonally up to a third-floor entrance where that large arch is. It is easy to trace the angle of those stairs because it is echoed in the facade decoration. This is only a part of a complex that included another wing, and was damaged during the 1571 razing of Moscow by the Tartars.

In search of a northwest passage to Asia, the first English envoys arrived via storm. Their ships were driven to the White Sea coast, where they were welcomed by Russians and then transported to Moscow for an audience with the czar. "Our men beganne to wonder at the Majestie of the Emperour," Captain Richard Chanceler reported. "His seate was aloft, in a very royall throne, having on his head a Diademe, or Crowne of golde, apparelled with a robe all of Goldsmithes worke, and in his hande he helde a Scepter garnished, and beset with pretious stones."

The czar gave the unexpected Englishmen an attentive welcome and lavished valuable trade privileges on them in the hope of making an ally out of the island-nation. He was so enamored of England that he would inquire as to Elizabeth's availability for marriage; that refused, he would line up asylum for himself in the event that he lost his throne. A whole series of English ambassadors wrote reports published in the 1560s by Richard Hakluyt in *Principall Voyages and Discoveries of*

the English Nation, read by Shakespeare (it perhaps inspired his use of "Muscovites" in *Love's Labor's Lost*), and
still an important source in sixteenth-century Russian
history.

Their "special relationship" with Ivan did not exempt
the English from the treatment accorded all foreign em-
issaries: travel about the city was only with permission
and under escort; residences were surrounded by high
fences with watchmen burning fires at night to stop anyone's sneaking out unnoticed; and informers keeping
constant records. Even by the rough standards of the age,
foreigners deemed Muscovites paranoid.

Looming right behind us is the **Rossiya Hotel**. Built
in 1967, it destroyed a huge portion of Kitai Gorod and
blights the skyline. But if you're hungry, thirsty, or in the
shopping mood and have a foreign passport to show the
entrance guards, it is a useful stop. Even if the restaurants
are closed, ask at information which floors have open
cafés. There you can get sandwiches, tea, pastries, and
sometimes coffee very inexpensively for rubles. On the
ground floor, on the side of the hotel overlooking the
Moskva River, is the entrance to a Beriozka hard-currency
shop. Here you'll find china, furs, liquor, books, crystal,
and other souvenirs that are all but unavailable in ruble
stores. But take care, the prices marked in rubles are ex-
changed at the old, much less favorable, rate.

Once restored, step out to the driveway on the side
of the hotel farthest from Red Square. A few hundred feet
back are fragments of the once-grand **Kitai Gorod Wall**
(1535–38). Anchored at two of the Kremlin corners, it
ringed the eastern part of the city with twelve towers, for
a total length of two and a half kilometers. The wall itself
was so wide that chariots could be driven along the shel-
tered top, the more quickly to resupply troops under
siege. At the ends of each of the main Kitai Gorod streets
was a massive gate allowing passage out. The snaking
walls, towers, and gates added much beauty to the Moscow panorama, but beginning in the eighteenth century

sections were taken down, with a culmination in the 1930s and 1950s, when the wall was reduced to its current state.

Return now to the driveway in front of the Old English Embassy. To your right (with your back to the hotel), and slightly up the hill, is the **Church of Maksim the Blessed** (#8 Varvarka). It stands on the site of an earlier fourteenth-century church where the *yurodivy* Maksim was buried, whence the current name. What you see now are the mutilated remains of a building raised in 1698 under the patronage of rich traders.

The entire complex of five buildings farther to the right is associated with the Romanov family, which ruled Russia for over three centuries, from 1613 until the 1917 Revolution. The belltower was built in 1784–89 in the place of an older version, which had been connected to the tall brick Znamensky Cathedral across the road to the right.

Step inside the looping road and walk toward the buildings set up against the Varvarka. On the left is a friary (1675–78) and on the right is the **Romanov Palace** (lower floor circa 1500; upper floor 1674).

Constant surveillance and fear of arrest were the lot of even powerful families in Russia, especially in the decades before the Romanovs managed to seize the throne. With the death of Fyodor I in 1598, the Rurikid dynasty (dating back to the ninth century) had died out, and the boyars vied for the prize of the throne. Boris Godunov managed to win in a vote held by the Zemsky Sobor (National Assembly) against competitors that included the Romanovs. Without ancestral title he was vulnerable to attack and intrigue, but he did strike back. In 1601 he broke up the Romanov family, which was ringleading the opposition, by planting roots and herbs in their storage basement and then accusing them of the extremely serious charge of witchcraft. The family was defeated, but unlike Ivan the Terrible, Boris Godunov rarely executed fallen enemies. Exile to monasteries was his preferred method, and the family patriarch, Fyodor, was forced to renounce the throne forever and to become a monk with the new name of Philaret.

In the end it did the Godunov family little good, since Michael Romanov, son of Fyodor, was elected to the throne in 1613 and established Russia's last dynasty with his father serving as patriarch. The palace was restored in the mid-nineteenth century as part of the Museum of the Romanov Boyars, and now serves as a museum of boyar life in general.

Next door to the left (facing the Varvarka) is the **friary** that served the Znamensky Monastery, founded by the Romanov family in 1629. You'll notice how similar in style it is to the Old English Embassy, with peaked roof and long eaves. The wooden stairway is close to what once served the English residence.

The colorful one-story building (on the other side of the Romanov house) with the green copper roof and red, yellow, and blue triangular decorations was part of the residential complex. Inside its fenced-in garden is an entrance to the **Museum of the Romanovs** (also established in the nineteenth century), which has been under renovation and will soon open.

Znamensky Cathedral (1679–84) stands back closer to the hotel within the encircling road. Like many other churches in Kitai Gorod, it got its start as a small domestic chapel, in this case on the Romanov estate. Notice the large windows decorated by colonnettes, decorative brickwork, and the five ornate cupolas.

Keep this cathedral in mind as we clamber up the steps on the right to the Varvarka (as we face it) to the **Church of St. George on Pskov Hill** (1657), which is illustrated on the cover of this book. Like the Znamensky Cathedral, this building is very typical of the mid- to late seventeenth century, in which Western decorative details begin to enter and modify the old forms (the adjoining belltower was built in 1818). The two churches are more similar than they first appear. Notice that they both have five tightly drawn cupolas perched on top of a boxlike volume (a traditional Russian feature), but that the large windowframes are decorated with columns. Perhaps the similarities are clearer if you visualize the Znamensky Cathedral painted red with white detailing, as it probably was originally.

The other thing to sense is how different both of these churches are from St. Basil's: they lack the central *shatyor* ("tent" spire), even if they reveal the same love for encrusted ornament. We are looking at buildings with a much simpler, more rectangular layout than that of St. Basil's. These seventeenth-century churches seem to exist to thrust out wonderful decorative details, but they lack the divine rhythm of the cathedral spires on Red Square.

Part of the reason is that the newer structures followed a several-decade interruption in stone building of churches, caused by economic ruin and the Time of Troubles. In other words, seventeenth-century architecture is more a revival than a continuation of past tradition, even if it is unmistakably Russian. But the bigger reason is church hostility to the tent form, culminating in a 1655 edict banning it altogether. Architects had to work within the format decreed by law: rectangular shapes with apses and one, three, or five cupolas. Thus bounded, they poured their creative energy into decorative effects. Such intense focus on surface was also congenial to the age, which was less spiritual than the sixteenth century.

We now visit perhaps the preeminent example of this seventeenth-century decorative style. To get there, turn left (with your back to Red Square) off the Varvarka immediately after the Church of St. George onto Ipatevsky Lane. Mount a steep hill. On the right is a spectacular vision of red brickwork, white cornices, green domes, tiers of *kokoshniki* and windows, and galleries and towers, all outlined by white relief carving against red.

Although the **Church of the Trinity on Nikitnikov**

Lane (1635–53) predates the 1655 building edict, it perfectly embodies the decorative ideals of the seventeenth century. It is an amalgam of old and new: the five-domed center and cubic chapels are reminiscent of the fifteenth century architecture that the church approved, but their arrangement is radical.

You may have noticed how often churches are mounted on a high platform (known as a *podklet*, literally a basement) so that you have to walk up steps to get to the entrance. One example of this technique, which had the effect of raising the height of the church, was the Annunciation Cathedral (Walk 1) in the Kremlin. That platform is here transformed into a lengthy arcade between the peaks of church and belltower. This space was vaulted over in a manner characteristic of civil architecture, which found wide rooms useful for large assemblies of people. In other words, the venerable *podklet* was adapted so that the church and belltower could be combined. This multiplied decorative possibilities because architects could play with more complex shapes than offered by a simple rectangular church with an apse and cupolas.

Nevertheless, this design is additive in principle rather than crystalline or even organic, as were the "tent" churches. The confectionary effects of the seventeenth century are delightful, but their sweetness does not beguile a taste for the spiritual. Sixteenth-century churches do not taste sweet, but their light shines brighter.

The elaborate windowframes, bizarre columns, and floral relief carving in front of us suggest an earthly paradise. To be fair, if decoration ever leads humans toward God, the spell is here. Look at the fluid and naturalistic carving around the windows and door portals. The builder, Grigory Nikitnikov, was a very rich merchant who loaned money even to the czar. He hired the same craftsmen who had worked on the Terem Palace in the Kremlin to carve the twisting laceworks of stone and wood, and the finest painters of the day to cover the walls with fresco and fill the iconostasis.

The Church of the Trinity on Nikitnikov Lane

The interior of the Church of the Trinity is almost perfectly preserved, and is open to the public from 10:00 A.M. until 6:00 P.M. daily, except for Wednesday, when it is closed, and Thursday, when hours are noon until 8:00 P.M.

Simeon Ushakov, who worked in the Annunciation Cathedral, was responsible with several other Kremlin masters for the interior frescoes (1652–53). Canonical restraints on painting had greatly loosened, hence there are many naturalistic details of the sort that caused battles only decades before, and that symbolize the encroachments of the West. To the right of the main altar is a small chapel that served as tomb to the Nikitnikov family. As you enter look at the opposite wall above the window for a very dramatic *Stoning of St. Stephen*. The painted floral passages throughout wonderfully echo the carved portals and the iconostasis frame. The church surges from stone flower to painted narrative, each amplifying the other.

It might be a good idea to rest in front of the altar, where often there are chairs, for a few minutes before we press on. We are going to leave the Kitai Gorod of distant times and briefly enter the modern commercial Kitai Gorod of the late nineteenth and early twentieth centuries. Just one block away, running parallel to the Varvarka, is the old financial district of Moscow.

To get there we retrace our steps down Ipatevsky Lane to the Varvarka. On the way up your eye was probably caught by the brick house on the corner with white *kokoshniki* and columns framing the windows (**#12 Ipatevsky Lane**). It was built in the middle of the seventeenth century and twenty years later given to the painter Simeon Ushakov as a studio.

At the Varvarka make a right, heading back the way we came, and at the second street, Fish Lane (Rybniy Pereulok), turn right. Running the entire length of the block on the left is the **Old Shopping Arcade** (Stariy Gostinniy Dvor), this portion of which was built in 1825–30. On the right side of Fish Lane is the **New Shopping**

Arcade (Noviy Gostinniy Dvor), built in 1838–40 to replace the fish market. The territory from here to Red
Square was once filled with wooden market stalls, divided into rows on the basis of product. Over the centuries stone buildings have replaced the incendiary
marketplace, but at the same time have preserved the
original function of the rows.

At the end of the block is the **Ilinka** (which recently
had its name changed back from Kuibishev Street), one
of the three main avenues in Kitai Gorod. To the left it
leads directly to the Savior Gate of the Kremlin. In fact,
each of Kitai Gorod's three main thoroughfares lines up
with a Kremlin tower, testimony to the days when Red
Square did not exist and two additional gateways led
through the parapeted walls.

The Ilinka was the business center for Moscow's merchant families, the place where their money was stored,
loaned, and borrowed, and where stocks were floated
and business was discussed. On the right corner of Fish
Lane and the Ilinka is the **Old Stock Exchange**, built in
classical style by M. D. Bykovsky in 1873–75, and now
serving the USSR Chamber of Commerce. The stock exchange members were the wealthiest men in the city,
obsessed with profit and given to speculation.

It's all the more strange that one of the stock exchange directors emerged as an early and most discerning
collector of modern art. Sergei Shchukin amassed the finest single collection ever of Matisse and Picasso, and also
bought Manet, Pissarro, Sisley, Renoir, Degas, Monet, van
Gogh, and Gauguin—at a time when these artists were
highly controversial even in the West. His early support
of Picasso was especially daring; what is more, he opened
his home to impoverished, radical young Russian artists
like Kasimir Malevich and Mikhail Larionov, who would
help pioneer the way into abstract art. After the Revolution, his home (Trubetskoy Palace, which his father had
bought from one of the oldest families in Russia) and the
collection were nationalized, but Shchukin continued to

provide the Bolshevik authorities with information and advice about its upkeep from his exile in Paris. Many of his paintings are now on view in the Pushkin Museum of Art.

Spreading in front of the stock market is the **Ilinka Square** (which recently had its name restored from Kuibishev Square), into which you should continue straight. The spare six-story building on the right side of the square (whose four lower stories are faced in columns of light brick crowned by tiny "orders" of garlands with sea horses) was built in 1904 by Fyodor Shekhtel, the best architect of Russian art nouveau. The building, which served as the Ryabushinsky Bank, is a good deal more utilitarian than the fanciful mansions he did for Moscow's millionaires. The top floor is an addition to the original building. Without it the proportions are more pleasing, but even so the stripped-down facade unifies exterior with function, a tendency that would strengthen in coming decades. On Walk 4 we'll be entering another of Shekhtel's creations, the Ryabushinsky Mansion of 1900, whose spectacular ironwork, asymmetry, fresco, and interior woodwork make the bank look especially austere by comparison.

The Ryabushinsky family, which derived its income from cotton, paper, and their bank, was one of the wealthiest in Moscow. Like Sergei Shchukin, Pavel Ryabushinsky was a director of the Moscow Stock Exchange and had radical taste in art. It is of nineteenth-century merchants like them that the actor Konstantin Stanislavsky, himself from such a family, wrote "the generation to which my parents belonged consisted of people who had already crossed the threshhold of culture although they had not received the benefits of higher education. . . . Numberless schools, hospitals, asylums, nurseries, learned societies, museums and art institutions were founded by their money, their initiative and even their creative effort."

Yet such philanthropy was not always the rule, and

merchant society was also a bastion of conservativism and support for the monarchy. Parents (who in some cases had raised themselves from serfdom) fought with their multilingual, effete offspring over money, politics, and religion. The younger members of merchant dynasties often felt alienated by the ruthless business tactics of their parents and grandparents. Suicides among them were common. Savva Morozov killed himself in France after his mother (an ex-serf) fired him for wanting to give a bonus to textile workers after one of their most profitable years ever; Sergei Sergeevich Shchukin (son of the great art collector mentioned earlier) drowned himself in the Moskva River at age 17; his uncle poisoned himself in Paris when he discovered that his vast collection of Goyas and El Grecos were forgeries and that he could not meet the demands of his creditors.

Sensitivity seems to have mingled with brute ambition in the merchant blood, a combination of qualities that led simultaneously to rapid economic growth, cultural flowering, cynicism, and both reactionary and radical politics. A perfect symbol of the age, Sergei Tretyakov, scion of a massively wealthy family, was shot by the Germans in 1918 for spying for the Bolsheviks.

Ilinka Square and Staropansky Lane, which turns off to the right, were where many countries had their embassies in the sixteenth and seventeenth centuries. Continue straight across the square. We follow the **Ilinka** (formerly Kuibishev) **Proezd**, which runs as if it were a continuation of Fish Lane. *Proezd* means "passage," and this street will take us through to Kitai Gorod's third main thoroughfare, Nikolskaya (formerly Twenty-Fifth of October) Street.

Half a block down the Ilinka Proezd on the left side are the remains of the **Bogoyavlensky Monastery**, in its day a lovely example of a style known as Naryshkin (or Moscow) Baroque. Now the Bogoyavlensky Cathedral's single cupola is missing and it is under restoration, but enter the yard. There are lessons here. The monastery

Residence of the abbot of Bogoyavlensky Monastery

was founded in 1292 on the edge of the forest to defend the eastern approaches to the Kremlin, before Kitai Gorod was fortified.

The decapitated cathedral in the center of the yard was built in 1693–96, and though it may seem vaguely similar to the Church of the Trinity on Nikitnikov Lane, it actually absorbs more of the West. The stone ornament around the windows, the pilasters, and the cornices are classical forms rather than ripe floral patterns. From Western texts with architectural drawings, Russian designers were adapting current Western ornament into their own version of baroque. Another telltale sign of this newer style is the octagon crowning the main body of the church. On top of it was a smaller octagon that supported a ribbed cupola. This was a lovely adaptation from the outlawed "tent" forms, with the exception that here the octagon does not taper to a point.

This is a very long way from the churches on Cathedral Square. The Bogoyavlensky Cathedral is very unlike the churches of old, in which cavelike spaces were raised for fresco and meditation. The huge windows here admit much light. It would even be fair to say that they symbolize a less introspective view of life.

The long building behind housed the monks, and the abbot's residence was to the right, both built at the same time as the cathedral and all designed as an ensemble.

Now walk back out onto the Ilinka Proezd and continue the final half-block until you reach the busy **Nikolskaya Street**. It has its origins in the pre-Mongol period. In other words, it is as old as the city itself, even though it long wore as a name the date of the Bolshevik Revolution, the twenty-fifth of October.

Across the street from us slightly to the right at #15 is the **Old Printing House**, pale blue with neo-Gothic tracework of white stone, sundials, spires, and a prancing lion and unicorn above the main entrance. It was built in 1811–15 by architect Ivan Mironovsky, and the plaque on the facade reads: "On this spot stood the printing yard where in 1564 Ivan Fedorov printed the first Russian book." This structure bears little resemblance to the original stone building, surrounded by the wooden huts of the pressmen. The unicorn and lion were the heraldic emblems of the press, carved into the original wooden gate that led into the courtyard—hence the stone version on the building facade.

While the idea of printing books may sound rather innocuous, intrigue surrounded every step of setting up a press in Russia, and it was only the combined efforts of Ivan the Terrible and Metropolitan Makary that brought it about. Primarily, they wanted to eliminate mistakes in religious texts that resulted from recopying over generations. The new press was combined with an attempt to do fresh translations of religious texts from Greek. But the brilliant Greek monk Maksim, hired to do the work, got prison for his efforts when he was convicted of faulty translation, by priests jealous of his authority. Twenty-five years later he was released and his translations became canonical; yet he was never allowed

Base of a column of the Old Printing House

to return to Greece; the Russian authorities felt that he had seen too much and would carry negative reports out with him. Scribes also found the idea of a press objectionable and incited an angry mob to burn it down. After Makary died, printing ended in Russia for nearly half a century.

Inside the courtyard, which can be reached through the Printing House's main gate, is the **Teremok**, a small palace restored in the 1870s in the manner of a seventeenth-century noble's residence. The jug-shaped columns at the entry porch covered by a "tent," checkerboard copper roof, window *kokoshniki*, and red and white detailing are all highly typical, as are the interior frescoes. The interior, now inaccessible owing to restoration, has two floors lying beneath the asphalt, which gives some indication of how over centuries debris and repaving cover yards of history. In the Teremok basement is a well, a phenomenon very common in private houses. In this area it would have been particularly easy to strike water because the Neglinnaya River, washing up from the Kremlin, flowed not far away.

The building is not simply a piece of seventeenth-century history, but an example of late-nineteenth-century revivalism as well. Artists and scholars studied traditions, practiced restoration, and began using old forms in an avant-garde manner. Mussorgsky, Diaghilev, Stanislavsky, Rimsky-Korsakov, Rachmaninoff, Kandinsky, Shaliapin—the list of cultural giants touched by Russian revival is almost endless, and here we have a little outbreak, tucked in a quiet courtyard off a busy street in Kitai Gorod.

Pass back out into the din and crowds of Nikolskaya Street and walk into the next block. At #7 enter the courtyard. On your right is the **Zaiconospassky** (literally, Behind the Icons Savior) **Cathedral**, named for the once nearby icon-trading stalls. This is where fifteenth- and sixteenth-century painters preferred spending their time in pursuit of private commissions, over underpaid work in the Kremlin. Though it is obscured by a ramshackle columned gallery, this church is a fairly pure example of Moscow Baroque, with classical orders, successive octagons mounted on the lower cube, and very large windows that would have been appropriate in a Viennese palace of 1700. The cathedral was raised in 1701–09 as part of a monastic complex by the same name, one of the oldest in Moscow.

The monastery buildings flanking the cathedral to the left were built around the same time and housed the **Slavic-Greek-Latin Academy**, Russia's first institution of higher education, begun late in the seventeenth century. Mikhail Lomonosov—Russia's most famous educator, founder of Moscow University, and creator of the rules of modern Russian—was a student resident of the corniced buildings.

These tranquil courtyards hidden off noisy streets give a view of what life centuries ago was like. The palace and *dvor* (courtyard) or cathedral and *dvor*, or government office and *dvor*, with accompanying buildings hemming in a semiprivate space, was a standard architectural arrangement that exists now only in quiet fragments.

The closer we get to Red Square, and we are very

close now, the more deeply we enter the territory of the old wooden trading rows, segregated by product and susceptible to fire. In 1500 we would have been surrounded by wood: shanties, mansions and *lavki* (tiny stores), with an occasional and magnificent stone building punctuating the skyline and overawing the street. Now all is stone, including the stalls which have been thrust indoors.

GUM (pronounced *goom*—the acronym means Government Department Store) is the stone-and-steel version of these rows, with three arcaded stories covered by massive skylights running the length of the building. It is still one of Moscow's main shopping centers, and well worth some browsing. You can enter from Nikolskaya Street right before it meets Red Square. In 1894 the architect A. N. Pomerantsev linked new construction methods with the old layout of rows (already long replaced by stone buildings), into a structure whose utility is apparent in seconds. Foot traffic flows easily and there is room for innumerable shops. The facade revives seventeenth-century ornamental motifs, and was designed to harmonize with the spired, red brick **Historical Museum** (1873–83) catty-corner. GUM has many exits; keep your sense of direction and try to find your way out onto Red Square.

It is amazing how well the varied ensemble on Red Square works, especially when you include **Lenin's Tomb**, whose austere modernity contrasts with the elegant teeth and bastions of the Kremlin, the spires of St. Basil's, and the revivalism of the newer buildings. The tomb was built from 1924 to 1930 in constructivist style by Alexei Shchusev, who had a long career back through art nouveau stretching behind him, including a church commissioned by the Grand Duchess Elizabeth who was killed by the Bolsheviks. Shchusev's monument repudiates traditional ornament as unnatural to the modern age,

The Cathedral of the Savior Behind the Icons

which makes this, as architecture anyway, an honest
building. It is rather strange to think that Shchusev's original plan in 1924 called for a small cube to be surmounted by four columns and an entablature—an
arrangement reminiscent of classicism. The tomb was rebuilt in wood, until the final stony form was fixed in
1930.

Lenin's embalmed body is on display Tuesdays,
Wednesdays, Thursdays, and Saturdays from 10 A.M. to
1 P.M., and Sundays from 10 A.M. to 2 P.M.. In the cata-
combs of the Monastery of St. Sophia in Kiev, embalmed
monks line the corridors, their gray, wrinkled hands visible folded over their shrouds. The holier the monk, the
more slowly his body was said to decay. The question of
what to do with Lenin's body was a huge dispute among
the Bolsheviks when he died, but their choice to enshrine
him in the flesh evokes centuries of precedent. It might
be well to take the chance to see him now. How much
longer he'll preside over Red Square, with democrats in
control of the Moscow City Council and the Russian Republic itself, remains to be seen.

The line to the tomb begins at the top of the Kremlin
Passage (Kremlevsky Proezd) on the other side of the
Historical Museum. Join the people lingering at the metal
fence. You will not be allowed to carry anything with you
into the tomb, including pocketbooks or cameras, but
there is an accessible checkroom in the Historical Museum with an entrance right onto the Kremlin Passage,
where you will be waiting.

Lenin's body is certainly one of the strangest monuments the Bolsheviks have left to their utopian ambitions.
Or perhaps it was very shrewd politics in a country just
beginning to leave its old faith, fields, and plows for fac-
tories in the cities.

Russia consistently manages to reveal itself in inad-
vertent symbols and gestures. The Czar Bell and Czar
Cannon (Walk 1) in the Kremlin are a perfect expression
of spiritual ambition and pride in power; the embalming

of Lenin reveals a need to find divinity in political leaders. When Andrei Sakharov died, priests told their congregations that he was *blazhenni* (blessed or holy), and we have seen how past grand dukes and czars joined the saints in church frescoes. Russia does not tend to divorce religion or philosophy from political life. For a man to be great, he has to make spiritual forces tangible.

Walk · 3

Novodyevichi Convent

Cathedral of Smolensk

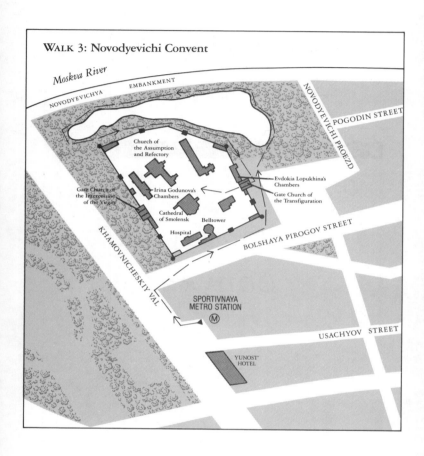

WALK 3: Novodyevichi Convent

Moskva River

NOVODYEVICHYA EMBANKMENT

NOVODYEVICHI PROEZD

POGODIN STREET

Church of the Assumption and Refectory

Gate Church of the Intercession of the Virgin

Irina Godunova's Chambers

Evdokia Lopukhina's Chambers

Gate Church of the Transfiguration

Cathedral of Smolensk

Belltower

Hospital

KHAMOVNICHESKIY VAL

BOLSHAYA PIROGOV STREET

SPORTIVNAYA METRO STATION Ⓜ

USACHYOV STREET

YUNOST' HOTEL

Starting Point: Entrance to Novodyevichi Convent

Walk Length: 2 hours

Metro Stop: Sportivnaya (Red Line). The metro is a short walk from the convent. On exiting, walk straight until you reach the street named Khamovnicheskiy Val just ahead. Make a right, and after a long block another right onto Bolshaya Pirogovskaya Street. The walls of the convent should be visible to the left. Walk the length of Pirogovskaya wall until the parking lot opens on the left, where you will find the entrance. The important thing is to walk right after exiting the subway. Novodyevichi Convent is hard to miss.

The Novodyevichi Convent is closed Tuesdays and the last day of each month. Regular hours are from 10:00 A.M. to 5:30 P.M., although from November 1 through April 30 closing is at 5:00 P.M. The tickets required for entry into the convent's churches and museums are available at the kiosk immediately to the left after you pass through the main entrance.

Since there are no cafés or restaurants in the convent, you might want to combine the walk with reservations at U Pirosmani (#4 Novodyevichi Proezd—247-1926), a cooperative restaurant specializing in Georgian food. From your table you'll have a wonderful view of the red and white parapets and gilded cupolas.

One of the best stocked hard-currency Beriozka stores is on Bolshaya Pirogovskaya Street, on the right just beyond the turn-off to Novodyevichi. Many people combine a visit to the convent with shopping. The store is closed Sundays.

To the left of the subway entrance is the Yunost' (Youth) Hotel for Soviet tourists. It has a café on the ground floor that serves inexpensive coffee and pastries for rubles.

The Novodyevichi Convent was founded in 1524 as a celebration of the capture of the ancient Russian city of Smolensk from Lithuania. Vasily III was ruler of Muscovy at that moment and like his father, Ivan III, he was an enthusiastic builder. It was appropriate that he mark one of the great victories of his reign with homage to God. Novodyevichi's stone Cathedral of Smolensk (1524–25) is the only building in the complex that dates from this founding period, and its five wide cupolas and austere whiteness are a contrast to the flaming Moscow Baroque churches and walls that surround it. With the early cathedral as a contrasting melody, the convent is a symphony of Moscow Baroque architecture at its decorative height.

Novodyevichi literally means "new maidens," although some of its inmates were neither new nor maidens. The regimen at the convent was strict, at least in theory, but some of the nuns were both very beautiful and unwilling occupants of the cloister. When the licentious False Dmitri II ruled from 1607 to 1610 he proved especially fond of these lovelies, and many pregnancies were noted at nunneries throughout Moscow. A company of *streltsy* was also stationed on the convent grounds, since it doubled as a fortress. While they were carefully segregated from the women, no doubt among them were intrepid lads who found their way to romance.

We begin at the **Gate Church of the Transfiguration** (1687–88), which sits atop the arched passageway into the convent grounds. In a way the gate itself resembles the *podklet* (literally, a basement), which Moscow churches often used as a platform, as with the Cathedral of the Annunciation in the Kremlin. Another very traditional feature is those scallop shells perched above the cornice. Remember the Cathedral of the Archangel in the Kremlin (Walk 1), which imported that Venetian motif? Here it is again. But taken as a whole the building doesn't look anything like those Kremlin predecessors. This church is a perfect example of Moscow Baroque architecture, which used the obligatory old motifs but rearranged them in a symmetrical, more Western manner.

Moscow Baroque has a quintessentially Russian appearance. But it is also the product of the destruction of an earlier tradition: the "tent" architecture of the sixteenth century, which culminated in St. Basil's Cathedral on Red Square (Walk 2). The tall "tent" spires that distinguish this style were a radical innovation that quickly earned the love of common people. But conservative clerics could find no precedent for the form. Finally in 1655 Patriarch Nikon mustered the strength to denounce this "corruption" of the tradition: "tent" churches were outlawed; the Cathedral of the Assumption at Vladimir again became the model for building, and one, three, or five cupolas were required.

Nevertheless, Moscow Baroque is perfect in its own way, perfectly decorative. It is the Russian echo of Western Baroque. Spirituality is not the issue. Returning our attention to the Gate Church, we see that it indeed has the canonical five cupolas. But there is irony in this obedience. By outlawing a style that was purely Russian, the church opened the floodgates to Western influence. Moscow Baroque architecture reveals a gradual absorption of more and more Western motifs. Look at the carved decoration above the windowframes. Russian builders were studying foreign architectural books and adopting the elements they liked.

Far more important than external decoration is a shift in the way the entire building, inside and out, is conceived. Symmetry is the rule. In this case we come across no unexpected chapels, belltowers, or other extensions that might induce the sense of organic growth. Most of the beauty of the church lies in its external ornament. It is very outward-looking. Twenty years later in St. Petersburg, Russians would begin making buildings almost identical to what was being done in the West. Moscow Baroque laid the groundwork with highly rational and organized interiors.

Before we enter the convent, we are going to take it in from a distance. Make a right to round the corner of the monastery wall, and spend a few minutes to stroll around the pond in front of you. As you look back over your shoulder, you'll see from the far left the Gate Church of the Transfiguration, the Belltower (1689–90), the Cathedral of Smolensk, and the Church of the Assumption (1685–88), punctuated by red-and-white bastions. The white, the gold, the red, and the ornate brickwork are reflected in the pond on placid days. This walk is a luxury the nuns were almost never permitted. Only on feast days were they allowed to circumambulate the walls and reenter. From the far end of the pond notice how well all the buildings harmonize. Ensemble creations are a strength in Russian architecture, and the methods changed much less than the style of individual buildings. The convent is carefully conceived so that its decorative walls lie below the glistening cupolas and tiers of church and belltower, just as the Kremlin was designed 200 years before.

Novodyevichi's greatest patron was Princess Sophia Miloslavskaya, the half-sister of Peter the Great, who ruled as regent during his minority. She was a ruthless woman with, in the words of one diplomat, "a deformed body, monstrously fat, a head as big as a bushel basket, hair on her face, and ulcers on her legs." When the ten-year-old Peter I was chosen czar on the death of Fyodor III in 1682, Sophia contrived a bloody revolt of the *streltsy* that resulted in a double coronation of Peter with his retarded half-brother Ivan V. Their double throne is on view in the Kremlin Armory. Ivan would have precedence as the first of the two czars, and Sophia would rule as regent.

For seven years Sophia was able to wield the power of czarina while Peter lived in near exile in the country with his mother, transported periodically to the Kremlin to participate in ceremonial affairs of state. The would-be czarina's most important building project was the Novodyevichi Convent. It is an irony of fate that it later served as her prison. Almost as soon as those elegant red brick and white stone battlements and churches were finished, Sophia fell from power and was banished to Novodyevichi.

It happened over several weeks in August and September 1689. Roused from bed in the middle of the night by the fearful rumor that *streltsy* assassins were on their way to murder him, Peter fled from his country retreat to the fortified monastery of Zagorsk. There, supporters rallied to his side, and gradually Sophia's regiments of *streltsy* themselves wavered and fled to Peter, pleading for mercy. Peter was, after all, czar, even if one of two, and the feeble-minded Ivan was no participant in the power struggle. Sophia's power base disintegrated. Her job as regent was conditional on the weakness and youth of the czars. Now the seventeen-year-old Peter was demanding power and there was nothing she could do to resist him.

Novodyevichi was not the end of Sophia, this time around anyway. She was not made a nun, and she continued to operate a network of informants who kept her acquainted with the politics of the Kremlin. Nevertheless, the company of black-robed Brides of Christ must have been a severe trial for the ambitious politician with blood on her hands. As we round the pond and continue toward the convent walls, don't forget that this panoramic view was usually forbidden to the inmates. They wandered inside those white walls, which lovely as they are, must have been bitter bane to all but the most spiritual of women.

Return now to the Gate Church of the Transfiguration and pass through the arched entryway. Just beyond is a little kiosk that sells tickets to the museums on the convent grounds. Ask for *vsye bilyeti* (all tickets). Immediately

Gate Church of the Transfiguration

to the left of the entrance, inside the grounds, is a red-and-white two-story building raised in 1687–88. These were the chambers of Evdokia Lopukhina, Peter the Great's first wife. Unlike his sister Sophia, she never intrigued against him, but he found her dull and conventional. So he availed himself of the traditional method of getting rid of an unwanted wife, and exiled her to a convent in Suzdal. Once she was committed, Peter was free to remarry, which he did to a servant girl (later empress) named Catherine. Peter hated the insipid Evdokia so much that he never trusted the son she bore him. Suspecting the lazy, drunken, self-indulgent fool of leading a conservative faction, Peter had him sentenced to death.

Peter the Great is famous for his founding of St. Petersburg and his fanatic desire to Westernize Russia. But in bloodthirstiness he was as bad as the worst of his predecessors. He delighted in participating in torture and executions, and would leap to wield the knout or axe on a victim. When investigation uncovered that his ex-wife Evdokia had taken a lover, the offending officer was impaled on a wooden stake up the anus and left to a lingering death that took over twenty-four hours. Evdokia escaped with a whipping and exile to an even more distant convent. But she would outlive Peter, and when her grandson came to the throne, she returned to the Kremlin, an honored dowager. Rather than participate in court life, she chose the cloister and ended her days in these chambers at Novodyevichi.

Plunging straight into the convent, we soon reach its heart, the regal white **Cathedral of Smolensk** (1524). It is very closely modeled on the Kremlin Cathedral of the Assumption (1475–79). Notice the five cupolas, and the pilasters supporting the wide arches peaking the facade. The arcaded gallery surrounding the base of the cathedral was an innovation that would prove very popular over the next two centuries. This cathedral achieves its power through restraint and the simple presentation of monolithic form. Its style is taciturn, and couldn't be further from the busy carving, tiering, brick patterns, and color contrasts of Moscow Baroque. Yet remember from the pond how well the cathedral integrated into the whole ensemble. This resonant white center is perfect counterpoint to baroque flame.

The frescoes inside were painted in the sixteenth century, beginning with the reign of Vasily III, hence they reflect the religious and political values of that moment. As in the Kremlin's Cathedral of the Assumption, the overarching theme is the unity of the Russian lands under the leadership of Muscovy. On the pillars facing the entrance as you walk in are the grand dukes of regions of the Kievan empire, later absorbed by Moscow: Vladimir, Tver, Kiev, and Chernigov. Towering above and behind the iconostasis is the fresco *Virgin of Smolensk*, for whom the church is dedicated. With the capture of Smolensk, Vasily III proved himself a worthy successor to his father, Ivan III.

Be sure to take a look at the icon immediately to the left of the altar gate, on the lowest level of the iconostasis. It is an early sixteenth century *Virgin of Smolensk* copied from an original that for once was returned to its city of origin. The later icon is said to have been carried into battle by the Russian forces that captured Smolensk, hence it holds an honored position as one of three key icons in the cathedral. Another striking icon is the *Virgin of Iberia* (1648), in which blood pours out of Mary's chin. It is a reference to a miracle that occurred during an unsuccessful siege of Constantinople. An icon hanging above a city gate was struck by an enemy lance, and then began to bleed. The siege was raised and success attributed to intervention by the Virgin.

Though the icons in the iconostasis date from the founding of the monastery, the gilt frame was produced in 1685 under the orders of Sophia. The fantastically opulent carving is testimony both to the skill of Russian carvers and to the flamboyant taste of the seventeenth century. The sincere and grueling piety of the icons is encased in a frame whose spectacular vines and tendrils reveal perhaps all too much love of the world.

Pass back through the arcaded gallery and outside. Directly across from us is the **Church of the Assumption** (1685–88) with an attached refectory. We are again going to experience the difference between the sixteenth and seventeenth centuries. First notice how similar the facade is to that of the Gate Church of the Transfiguration. The windows are heavily decorated with a similar pattern, and the corners are marked by the same double stripes of attached columns.

The entrance is around the corner to the left. This is an operating church, which means that women are expected to cover their heads. We will enter through what was once a dining hall for the nuns and now serves as a lengthy chapel leading up to the high altar. Smell the burning, crackling tallow. Hundreds of candles light the iconostasis and dozens of individual icons. It is strange how little the abundant gilt flashes. Instead the gold simply glows as if lit from within.

In the Cathedral of Smolensk the fresco covers all available surfaces. Here in the Church of the Assumption, panels of fresco are surrounded by decorative bands of carving. Each religious image is detached and presented as if it were an offering. We see not the unified cosmos of the cathedral but individual saints to whom homage is paid with ornament. There is piety in this decoration, but it is not as deep as the terrible directness of frescoes and icons in the older churches. Nevertheless, taken all together the gold, incense, smoky light, and singing have an overwhelming effect. The bass chant of the liturgy vibrating in the candlelight makes the theatrical baroque-style spiritual.

You may want to purchase a special prayer service for relatives or friends. Inside the entrance to the church old women sell thin red candles for 30 kopecks to 2 rubles each. You can purchase a candle, and place it, with a slip of paper naming the persons for whom you want prayer, in front of the appropriate saint. Or for several rubles you can have a separate service performed. Say to the candle lady *"za zdraviye"* (*za ZDRAV-ee-ye*) if the prayers are for the living, and *"za upokoi"* (*za oo-pah-KOY*) if they are for the dead. On the paper she gives you, write the names and get her to point where to leave it. *"Kudah?"* (*Koo-DAH*), meaning "Where?" should be sufficient to elicit an answer.

Outside lies a simple white building directly across from the church entrance. It is hard to believe it was the residence of a czarina, and one not even in disgrace at that. After the death of her husband, Czar Fyodor I in 1598, Irina Godunova declined the throne and voluntarily retired here. Because there was no heir, a national assembly had to vote on a new czar. Her brother, Boris Godunov, the most powerful boyar in Muscovy, "withdrew" himself from the race and retreated to Novodyevichi to live with his sister. When backers arranged his selection by the assembly, he refused to accept. Three times a procession of Muscovites came here to plead with Boris to ascend the throne before he finally agreed. He was named czar in the Cathedral of Smolensk, and formally crowned later in the Cathedral of the Assumption in the Kremlin. He didn't manage, however, to found a dynasty. Boris's son ruled for only a few weeks after his father's death before he was deposed by False Dmitri I.

As one of the richest monasteries in Russia, Novodyevichi was the repository of unmarriageable sisters, mothers, and old wives from noble families. They followed politics avidly, and the disgrace of another clan would lead to an influx of new recruits. The class system was as rigid inside the monastery as it was outside. A nun without any wealth could expect to work as a scullery maid and to receive no relief from the rigid rules governing behavior. For the truly pious the monastery answered all their needs, but for more ordinary women, cloistered against their will and without men, it was the site of rages and impotent political maneuvers.

An art nouveau chapel and burial vault
for the Prokhorov Family

Walk around the tree-shaded grounds. The convent is also the site of a famous cemetery dating from 1727, in which many notables are buried. The low white pavilion with a green roof next to the refectory is the **Mausoleum of Count Sergei Volkonsky** and his wife, Countess Maria. They spent thirty years' exile in Siberia for attempting to depose Czar Nicholas I in favor of a constitutional monarchy, along with a group of titled revolutionaries known as the Decembrists. Countess Volkonskaya could have stayed in Petersburg and lived the good life, since her exiled husband was legally "dead." But like several other Decembrist wives, she chose Siberia alongside her spouse. The Volkonskys were among the very few who survived until the amnesty of 1856. In a part of the cemetery usually closed to the public, Nikita Krushchev and Nadezhda Alleilueva (Stalin's wife, who committed suicide) are buried.

A 1770 painting of the monastery shows black, shapeless nuns walking purposefully about the monastery grounds. The chambers for noble nuns were also connected by wooden passageways to church entrances, and they were thus protected from prying eyes. This life was an extension of the *terem*, or women's quarters of secular life, out of which females were rarely permitted to stir. Even the middle classes protectively kept women shut up at home.

In the convent the women embroidered vestments and fabrics for sale. The most skilled worked with rare silk thread and cabochon jewels that were applied to priests' garments. During the service, emeralds and rubies would pick up the flickering light until the priest himself shone like a messenger from heaven. Life unfolded above all inside, within dark shimmering chapels flooded with incense, and within private cells where the only occupations were gossip, sewing, and prayer.

Be sure to walk below the battlements in your meanderings about the grounds. The defensive role of the monastery, which protected both the land and the river route to Moscow from the west, was never forgotten. During the Tartar sack of Moscow in 1571, Novodyevichi held out. Moscow is ringed by such monastery forts, which made more secure the precarious lives of Kremlin rulers.

On the pond side of the convent, nestled in the northern corner of the wall, is an innocuous white building with three chimneys. It harbored Princess Sophia after Peter the Great's rise to power. Like a mafia chieftain operating from prison, she maintained contacts with *streltsy* officers and conservatives dissatisfied with Peter's reforms. In 1697 she was about to strike when Peter was warned. Her closest allies were executed and the *streltsy* regiments exiled to the Polish and Turkish borders. Constant warfare on this "Eastern front" led to greatly shortened life spans, and Sophia's primary instrument of policy was removed. It is a wonder that Peter didn't kill her then and there. Perhaps he respected her relentless pursuit of power.

With the *streltsy* occupied in the East, Peter felt safe enough to go on a lengthy "grand tour" in the West, both to educate himself and to gather specialists for the modernization of Russia. While abroad, the *streltsy* sent a delegation to Moscow asking to return to the capital from the bloody frontier. Sophia encouraged them, perhaps with the intention of felling Peter, and they began to move en masse. Peter's foreign military advisers skillfully put down the uprising and waited for the enraged czar to return.

Vengeance was slow and thorough, since Peter was convinced that the march on Moscow was an attempt to unseat him. Literally thousands of *streltsy* along with their wives and relatives were systematically tortured. Sophia's maidservants were broken on the rack and one gave birth during interrogation. Victims were lashed, branded, torn with red-hot pincers, and revived by physicians for more. Peter personally participated in the exercise. As executions went forward, *streltsy* heads were mounted on pikes at the approaches to the city. In addition, one hundred ninety-seven of these Praetorians were hung at Novo-dyevichi and left to dangle and rot for five months. Three of the corpses hung in front of Sophia's windows close enough for her to touch them. Their putrefying hands held petitions for her to take power as regent for the son Peter hated. Even incense must have left unmasked the pervasive stench of decaying flesh. Sophia's political career was at an end, and she was finally forced to take the veil. She died five years later in 1704, and is buried in the Cathedral of Smolensk.

Walking under green, bending trees in the summer, or over a soft carpet of snow in the winter, it is hard to reconcile the avid cruelty of politics with the peace now reigning in the convent. The slender proportions of the churches and ribbed gold of the cupolas are an expression of Sophia's identity, too. After all, she chose to commission these buildings when she was in power. Is it too much to say that this sort of decoration, which is almost all surface, can disguise secret and much uglier passions? There is something about the glib beauty of Moscow Baroque that is frightening. St. Basil's Cathedral is frank in its terror, but seventeenth-century buildings glide over the truth in endless search of good taste.

With such questions on our minds, let's wend our way to the **Belltower** (1689–90). It is possible to think of Novodyevichi as a piece of music, with each cupola at a different height marking a note, the smallest serving as eighth notes and the largest as whole notes. There is music in the score. If the convent's cupolas were played, the belltower's gold would pierce the air with its high note. In a sense, that's bell-ringing. Taken as a whole the convent makes a lovely piece of music; under the peal of bells its excess becomes a prayer.

This is a poetic way of saying that Moscow Baroque is an art form of combined effects that, felt together, overwhelm. Inside a church we succumb to the charm of overwrought gilt made unearthly by votive candles. Outside, the rhythm of the domes against a changing sky is a silhouette as powerful as an early icon. But it is not luck or lighting that brings about this transformation. Moscow Baroque is better than it really should be because of the extremely high level of craft in the carving. Russia's craftsmen animated forms that hardly deserved their passion, and when the light strikes or the bells ring their prayers fly straight to heaven.

The architects were smart enough to leave these carvers room to work on windowframes, cornices, and attached columns. The belltower is very simple when you look at it: six octagons placed one on top of the other.

The Belltower

Open and blind arcades alternate and the bells are visible. This tower is a direct descendant of the Belltower of Ivan the Great in the Kremlin (Walk 1), which is also octagonal, although its tiering is less elaborate. The convent belltower makes apparent how dependent Moscow Baroque is on repetition. The same Western-style balustrade marks each tier, and the arcades are decorated with the patterns used on the windows. It harmonizes perfectly with the other churches.

With your back to the Smolensk Cathedral, immediately right of the Belltower is the old hospital to the convent, now a museum with paintings and applied art. It is very much worth a visit, for the vivid and psychological portraits of the seventeenth century alone. You'll also get a chance to see some of the textile, silver, and ceramic art produced in the monastery's workshops, or acquired through donation.

When you emerge, walk to the southern gate on your left. This is where we will begin to say farewell to the monastery with so much white stone flowering against red brick. Above is the **Gate Church of the Intercession of the Virgin** (1683–88), whose three cupolas and hexagonal shapes anticipate a later stage of Moscow Baroque. In the 1690s architects would begin working towers into their buildings, as if out of nostalgia for the *shatyor* spires of the sixteenth century. "Tent" churches were never to return, but late, or Naryshkin, Baroque did result in buildings whose sumptuousness has rarely been equaled. The Novodyevichi churches are more restrained, but taken in ensemble they match in opulence baroque effects anywhere in the world.

In order to exit the monastery, we will need to return to the northern entrance through which we came. Take your time on the way back through the grounds. Having read about the buildings, relax and let the ensemble work its peace. Try to imagine what the nuns living here dreamt as they strolled these paths.

The Novodyevichi Convent wall and bastions

Walk · 4

From the Arbat to Kachalova Street

A VIEW OF LITERARY MOSCOW

A wing of the Ryabushinsky Mansion

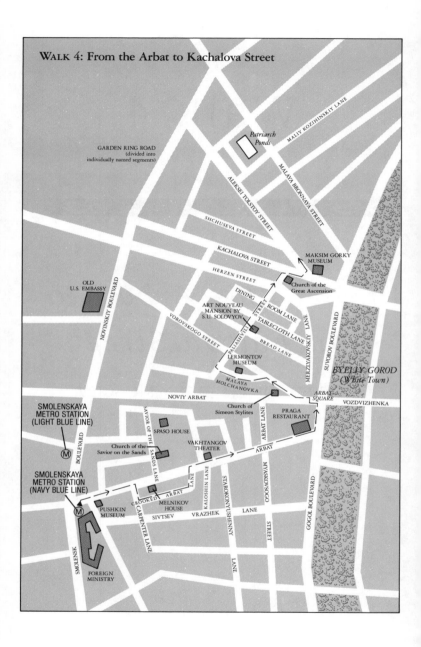

WALK 4: From the Arbat to Kachalova Street

GARDEN RING ROAD
(divided into
individually named segments)

Patriarch Ponds

MALIY KOZIHINSKIY LANE

MALAYA BRONNAYA STREET

ALEKSEI TOLSTOY STREET

SHCHUSEVA STREET

KACHALOVA STREET

MAKSIM GORKY MUSEUM

HERZEN STREET

Church of the Great Ascension

OLD U.S. EMBASSY

NOVINSKIY BOULEVARD

DINING ROOM LANE

PALASHEVITE STREET

ART NOUVEAU MANSION BY S.U. SOLOVYOV

TABLECLOTH LANE

VOROVSKOGO STREET

BREAD LANE

MERZLYAKOVSKIY LANE

SUVOROV BOULEVARD

BYELIY GOROD
(*White Town*)

LERMONTOV MUSEUM

MALAYA MOLCHANOVKA

NOVIY ARBAT

Church of Simeon Stylites

ARBAT LANE

ARBAT SQUARE

VOZDVIZHENKA

SMOLENSKAYA METRO STATION (LIGHT BLUE LINE)

Ⓜ

BOULEVARD

SAVIOR OF THE SANDS LANE

SPASO HOUSE

VAKHTANGOV THEATER

PRAGA RESTAURANT

ARBAT

Church of the Savior on the Sands

MYASKOVSKOGO

GOGOL BOULEVARD

SMOLENSKAYA METRO STATION (NAVY BLUE LINE)

Ⓜ

PUSHKIN MUSEUM

CROOKED ARBAT

MELNIKOV HOUSE

CARPENTER LANE

SIVTSEV VRAZHEK

LANE

KALOSHIN LANE

STAROKONYUSHENNY LANE

LANE

SMOLENSK

FOREIGN MINISTRY

Starting Point: The beginning of the Arbat on Garden Ring (Sadovoye Koltso) Road

Walk Length: 2 hours (not including time in museums)

Metro Stop: Smolenskaya (Light Blue or Navy Blue Lines). Both of the metro exits are on the Garden Ring (Sadovoye Koltso) Road, which is where the Arbat begins. The Navy Blue Line will leave you on the proper side of Sadovoye, literally adjacent to the Arbat. Walk straight out the exit and you will bump into it. The Light Blue Line will put you on the other side of Sadovoye. Walk out the exit and down the stairs to the underpass straight ahead, which will take you across Sadovoye. On the other side turn to the right (with your back to the street). The Arbat will open up on your left in one block.

There is also an Arbat metro stop (Arbatskaya). We don't recommend it because it will leave you at the wrong end of the Arbat for the purposes of this walk.

Monday and Tuesday are bad days to take this walk if you want to visit the literary museums along the way, which are closed then. Be careful toward the end of each month when museums are closed for cleaning, as noted. Ticket prices are nominal.

There are innumerable cafés, restaurants, and shops along the course of this walk. It is really just a matter of taking your pick. If you plan to eat, we suggest choosing beforehand based on the listings at the end of the book, and making reservations. There are many cafés along the Arbat that you can simply walk into; however, their offerings are limited.

The route from the Arbat to Kachalova Street will take us through some of Moscow's most expensive neighborhoods of the pre-Revolutionary period. This is a walk through the nineteenth century. Classical motifs dominate the facades of the older buildings we will pass, yet as the nineteenth century wears on an eclecticism takes over, which culminates in Moscow's romantic art nouveau mansions.

In this epoch, Russia lived in intimate proximity with foreign, especially French, culture. Much of the gentry spoke French, and the highest aristocracy spoke it far better than Russian. Well-educated people added English and German to their repertory of languages, and when the state permitted, they traveled abroad.

It has been fun to "read" earlier Russian architecture in psychological terms, but the nineteenth century resists such an approach. Neoclassicism is an international style, and its elegant harmonies do little to reveal the deepest views of those people residing within. To understand this age we have to turn to poetry, memoirs, novels—anything written. This walk is an exploration of literary salons bubbling with conversation and champagne, millionaires' mansions, and wide boulevards laid in the place of old fortress walls.

It is the Moscow of exhilaration after the 1815 occupation of Paris, which certified Russia as a great European power. Intoxicated by French liberalism, young army officers returned home with high hopes for Russia. Czar Alexander I, it was thought, surely would grant Western-style freedoms to his subjects as a reward for their loyalty in a desperate war. The reforms never came, and with Alexander's death these disappointed officers launched the 1825 Decembrist coup in pursuit of a constitutional monarchy.

The rebellion failed and its leaders were hung, so this is also a Moscow of bitter gloom and repression. It is the Moscow of Nicholas I, who ensured that every squeak of protest was punished and whose secret police patronized compliant journalists and endlessly recruited informers. Later in the century it is the center of the industrial revolution, when fabulous fortunes were won by common merchants who built landmark mansions; and still later, it is the site of barricades and gunfire during the 1905 Uprising. In the Soviet era, it is the Moscow of choice apartments handed out to the lucky. Ed Howard, the only CIA officer ever to defect, has an apartment in this neighborhood.

Standing at the top of the **Arbat** near the Garden Ring (Sadovoye Koltso) Road, which marked the city limits in the early nineteenth century, we have a nice sloping vista down the street. Way back in the fourteenth century, the Arbat hill was settled by traders and carriage makers who serviced the Kremlin-town, a nearby settlement through the forest and across two small rivers. The name Arbat is said to derive either from the Tartar word for carriage (*arbi*) or from the Arabic word for suburb, but no one is really sure, an uncertainty befitting one of Moscow's oldest streets. There is nothing left of this ancient period except the road itself. In the seventeenth century Czar Alexei renamed the Arbat "Smolensk Road," because it heads in the direction of this ancient city, but the new name was never accepted by Muscovites, who prize this street as a symbol of Old Moscow. The Arbat, it seems, will always remain the Arbat.

The massive fire of 1493, which devoured the city and led to the creation of Red Square, began nearby from a candle in the Church of Nicholas on the Sands. This church existed close to what is now the U.S. Ambassador's residence on Spasopeskovsky Pereulok (Savior of the Sands Lane). Later another great conflagration, the fire of 1812, destroyed the wooden structures that had been built up over intervening centuries down the Arbat and in its adjoining lanes.

Hence the architecture of the Arbat is a product of the nineteenth century, after it had become one of the city's toniest neighborhoods. In 1986, before he had become leader of the opposition, Moscow Mayor Boris Yeltsin forbade car traffic on the street and it was transformed into a pedestrian mall, a sort of Georgetown or Greenwich Village which attracts strollers, shoppers, peddlers, and artists from all over the city. Here you will not have trouble finding a café; you can also have your portrait painted, purchase used books, or buy an overpriced Palekh box (black, wooden, painted with a fairy-tale scene, and lacquered) from a seedy street entrepreneur. At night tight knots of pedestrians, undisturbed by the police, gather to debate religion and politics.

Whatever you do don't use dollars or any other foreign currency for your purchases. Nancy Reagan's hairdresser was arrested on the Arbat using U.S. cash to buy a souvenir. He spent several hours in jail before the Secret Service found out what had happened and sprang him. Unless you have comparable protection, it could make for an unpleasant experience.

We begin near the top of the Arbat at **#53**, where Alexander Pushkin spent his first three months of married life in 1831. Although changed, the mansion is typical in scale of the Empire-style architecture built in this area after the fire of 1812. In Pushkin's time the Arbat was a cobblestoned street with churches and belltowers rising high into the sky above the one- and two-story stone houses.

Pushkin's apartment is a museum with access through the gate on the right side of the building (open noon to 6:00 P.M. Wednesday, Thursday, and Friday; 11:00 A.M. to 5:00 P.M. Saturday and Sunday). Prints of Moscow in his era, portraits, and documents are displayed on the first floor, with period furniture (not belonging to him) on the second. In fact the museum is larger than his quarters were; he lived only on the second floor, which is now arranged more as a shrine than a residence.

Moscow in 1831, when Pushkin lived here, was a depressing place. All hope for liberal reform had been crushed with the Decembrist uprising just over five years before, and people distracted themselves with balls, duels, and amorous adventures.

Pushkin escaped involvement in the revolt mainly because he was in internal exile at the time it occurred, but almost all the main conspirators were friends of his. Lines from lyrics like the "Ode to Freedom," for which Pushkin had won his exile in the first place, were an inspiration to the rebels and an outrage to the government:

> O tyrants of the world, beware!
> And you, good men, take heart and dare—
> Arise, O fallen slaves!

The men who took heart were hung, and their followers exiled to the mines of Siberia from which few would emerge.

Yet when it came to Pushkin, the cunning Czar Nicholas forebore. He had other plans in mind. Several months after the coup attempt Pushkin received a cryptic message in exile where he was awaiting arrest: he was to travel forthwith to Moscow under escort, "not in the position of a prisoner," and present himself at the headquarters of the czar. Upon arrival, without changing, Pushkin reported as ordered to the Kremlin and, unprepared, was taken in to see his ruler.

"What would you have done if you had been in Petersburg on the fourteenth of December?" Nicholas asked his subject, referring to the date of the insurrection.

"I should have been in the ranks of the rebels," the poet answered.

Nicholas then asked whether he was willing to change his sentiments (which was what Pushkin had promised in frightened letters to interceding friends in the capital). Pushkin agreed, but complained about censorship, at which the ruler of Russia promised to be his personal censor. The poet was free to travel wherever he pleased within the empire with the exception of Petersburg, which would require permission. The audience at an end, Nicholas showed him into a room of courtiers and announced, "Gentlemen, here is the new Pushkin for you; let us forget about the old Pushkin." On the eve of his coronation, the soon-to-be czar was determined to show a compassionate face.

Pushkin was initially grateful but would soon discover that his special tie to the throne was a prestigious disaster. Until death the secret police would hound him for proofs of loyalty. When Pushkin took the liberty of reading new poems to a few friends, the chief of secret police got word and sharply chastised him for not having submitted it first. To his dismay Pushkin discovered that the czar's "personal" censorship extended not simply to published works but to everything.

Nevertheless, the meeting with the czar and his apparent pardon gave him great prestige in conventional circles. It was partly this new status that brought him a second disaster that leads us to this apartment: an expensive wife of stunning beauty but little intellect, who had trouble keeping the names of his books straight. Pushkin approached the conservative parents of Natalya Goncharova several times, but was refused. The impoverished old family hoped to trade a gorgeous daughter for a fortune. Pushkin became absolutely infatuated and, struck by the poet's seemingly rising star, the family finally agreed to the match.

"She was tall," an admiring count recorded, "with an incredibly thin waist, well-developed shoulders and bosom, and her small head, like a lily on a stalk, swayed gracefully on her slender neck; such a beautiful and perfect profile I have never seen, and then her complexion, eyes, teeth, mouth! Yes, she was a real beauty, and all other women, even the most attractive, faded when she appeared." Later she attracted the eager eye of the czar himself, which caused the poet no end of problems.

The marriage was held January 18, 1831, in the Great

Ascension Church, which we will see further along on this walk. Ten days later the newlyweds held a ball in this apartment that lasted until 3:00 A.M. Tempted by a wife with the appeal of Manon, Pushkin would return to the social whirl of dances, gambling, and duels. The couple lasted three months in Moscow before Pushkin managed to flee with the seventeen-year-old bride to semirural Tsarkoye Selo (Czar Village) outside of Petersburg. There, an interval of peace preceded his reentry into the maelstrom of the capital and his last, fatal duel.

Army officers, civil servants, and writers of the early nineteenth century were, like Pushkin, virtually all members of the aristocracy or gentry, and largely supported themselves off serf labor on distant estates. The Pushkin family estate was badly run and heavily mortgaged, so the poet was forced to rely on his pen for income. Russia's literature flowered in the midst of a class with a great deal of time on its hands. Imagine the settings of Jane Austen or Samuel Richardson, and then overlay political intrigue and fear of informers, and you get an idea of the Russian atmosphere of this period. Like their English counterparts, the Russian gentry concerned themselves with love, marriage, balls, and domestic routine, but for thinking people much more of life was politicized. The authority of the czar and the interest of the secret police extended into private realms that in England were subject only to town gossips, the local priest, and forbidding parents.

Return outside to the Arbat again, and continue down it until you reach **Plotnikov Pereulok** (Carpenter Lane) on your right, so named because carpenters lived in the area from at least the seventeenth century. Enter the lane. Immediately on your left is Krivoarbatsky Pereulok (Crooked Arbat Lane), which wends its way back to the Arbat at the other end. Down the lane on your left at #6 behind a wooden fence and partly masked by trees is **Konstantin Melnikov's house**, one of the great architectural monuments of the 1920s.

It is easy to forget that Russia from the end of the nineteenth century through the 1920s was at the forefront of modernist culture and helped revolutionize painting, music, ballet, opera, poetry, and architecture. Melnikov's house is a strange and wonderful constructivist building that is as expressive as it is geometric.

The front of the house is a rectangular frame of glass panes three stories high. The inscription at the top reads:

ARCHITECT

KONSTANTIN MELNIKOV

—a symbol of individual professional pride, rash for the period which saw the rise of Stalin. Behind this front the building curves like a cylinder. To the rear of this first cylinder is attached a second. Both cylinders are punctured by innumerable hexagonal windows at irregular levels. You can get a good view of the rear of the house, especially the wonderful windows, by walking into the back courtyard of the building on the right.

When Konstantin Melnikov built his home in 1927 (at low cost owing to his reliance on peasant building techniques), he was perhaps Russia's most famous architect. He had taken first place for design of the Soviet Pavilion at the Paris Exposition in 1925, and he went on to receive many commissions from the Moscow city government. While his work was read as constructivist, in fact he criticized the school as "soulless" and wrote that he strove for "those rare intimations of the unseen but real world of our feelings." Melnikov was at heart a symbolist and refused to join any of the factions that ripped apart the world of architecture on the eve of the purges, despite the fact that he was often the envied target of all. Amazingly, he survived to die a natural death in 1974 without having been arrested. His son, a painter, still lives in this house.

Continue down Krivoarbatsky until you reach the Arbat again. We have bypassed **Spasopeskovsky Pereulok**. If you want to see the U.S. Ambassador's grand residence (built in 1914 in neo-Empire style for a rich Siberian merchant), or the seventeenth-century Church of the Savior on the Sands (now a studio for production of cartoons), walk back up the Arbat half a block and make a right at the outdoor café with a fenced-in seating area.

Slightly farther down the Arbat (from where Krivoarbatsky enters) on your left at #26 is the **Vakhtangov Theater**. It was founded in 1921, but bombed during the war and replaced in 1947. Founder Yevgeny Vakhtangov was a student of Konstantin Stanislavsky, but evolved his own acting methods that are still taught in the theater's prestigious school. *Princess Turandot* by Carlo Gozzi, the play that made the reputation of the theater, is still part of its repertory. You can buy tickets at the box office inside.

Keep your eyes peeled as you walk. You may want to enter some of the numerous stores along the route, including *bukinisti* (which sell used and rare books), a commission shop for crystal and china (#32 Arbat), a Ukrainian bookstore, or Dom Plakati (House of Posters) farther down. At the bottom of the street artists do a lively business in quick portraits. Often the prices are posted in English; otherwise you can negotiate and take a seat in front of an easel. All up and down the Arbat other artists mount their wares on building walls and cleared spaces. Until several years ago this commercial activity was almost all illegal and the Arbat was a busy street of cars, trolleys, and buses.

At the bottom the street opens out into the wide Arbat Square. The far side of the square marks the beginning of **Byeliy Gorod** (White Town), which arches around the older Kremlin and Kitai Gorod areas like a huge horseshoe. This area of the city grew from these kernels. The White Town walls, long torn down, were raised in 1585–91, replacing earthen and wooden ramparts dating from the late fourteenth century. The Arbat Gate through the wall stood across the square to the right.

The small, odd pavilion on the far side of the square

Entrance to an art nouveau apartment building on Crooked Arbat Lane

is the entrance to the Arbatskaya subway station built in 1935. To the left of it, with the neon crown, is the **Khudozhestvenny (Artistic) Cinema**, dating from before the Revolution, which in 1930 showed the first "talkies" in Moscow.

In the early nineteenth century Moscow streets were watched over by gendarme posts, peculiar in the sense that each policeman made his home where he was sta-

tioned. The posts were one-room wooden or circular
stone buildings, outside of which wives grilled chickens
or hung the laundry. A Russian memoirist described vividly the figure cut by these guardians of order. They wore
beautiful gray uniforms, with red insignia on their collars,
spiked helmets, and cutlasses tucked into their belts—
perhaps an expression of Nicholas I's love of spiffy uniforms. They held halberds, "exactly like those supplied

to extras in theatrical productions about the Middle Ages," but their decorativeness went no further than dress.

"The policemen were unquestionably dirty, crude, glowering and ignorant," he recalled. "No one even considered turning to them for information. They were living 'scarecrows' for evil and good alike, so that on the street the public felt and saw with its own eyes the power of the authorities." Serf owners did find them useful, however, as instruments of punishment. When a serf had misbehaved he was sent to receive his thrashing, as prescribed by the owner, from these ever-ready enforcers of public morals.

The massive, century-old **Praga** (Prague) **Restaurant** at #2 Arbat on the left offers grand views from its balconies but less exciting food. Although the formal dining halls require reservations (tel. 290-6171), the café on the ground floor does not. It is decorated in a spare *moderne* style, and you serve yourself from a buffet. The main disadvantage is its popularity, which can mean long lines.

We are now going to cross the busy Noviy Arbat (New Arbat) to the left on the other side of the Praga Restaurant. At the intersection to the right (with your back to the Praga), the Noviy Arbat changes its name to the Vozdvizhenka (Street of the Exaltation of the Cross) and leads directly to the Trinity Gate of the Kremlin. Both the Noviy Arbat and the Vozdvizhenka made up what was **Kalinin Prospect** until recently, when the traditional names were restored. Mikhail Kalinin was one of the few old Bolsheviks to survive Stalin's purges and remain in power until he died in 1946, credentials which did not enamor the democratic Moscow City Council to the new name.

Perhaps the name Kalinin Prospect is more in keeping with the quality of the architecture now on the Noviy Arbat. To your left is a row of skyscrapers on both sides of the avenue. In the early 1960s, Krushchev had the street razed and widened for a more modern look. A huge number of old buildings in one of Moscow's loveliest quarters were destroyed.

The wooden Empire-style house of Lermontov's grandmother

One of the survivors of Krushchev's reconstruction is the **Church of Simeon Stylites** (1676–79). Cross the Noviy Arbat through the underpass, then walk up the other side of the avenue to the left. The five-cupola white church with attached belltower is plainly visible, set back from the street. Its style hearkens back to the first half of the seventeenth century and shows none of the Western influences that were creeping into Russian churches of this period. The whitewashed interior is now a museum of conservation.

Running directly behind the church is Malaya Molchanovka Street, where Russia's second greatest poet, **Mikhail Lermontov** (1814–41), lived with his grandmother from 1830 to 1832. Do not confuse Malaya Molchanovka with the wider Vorovskogo Street to the right—take what looks like an alley on the left. The house at #2 is now a museum (open 2:00 to 9:00 P.M. Wednesday and Friday; 11:00 A.M. to 6:00 P.M. Thursday, Saturday, and Sunday; and closed Monday and the last Saturday of each month). Inside are manuscripts, period furniture, and two rooms of Lermontov's extraordinary paintings and drawings. The building went up after the fire of 1812, and with the mezzanine topping a wide first story, it is typical of the Empire-style wooden architecture of the period.

When Pushkin and his diva were residing on the Arbat, Lermontov lived here as an adolescent with his grandmother. In 1831, at age 16, he wrote "Angel," one of the greatest short lyrics in Russian. "Through the midnight sky an angel was flying . . ." it opens, with a picture of a young soul in divine embrace being delivered to "the world of sorrow and tears." The soul languishes in the world, filled with a longing for the dimly remembered airs of heaven.

Yet Lermontov would also become a battle-wise cavalry officer, and an outstanding mathematician, musician, and painter before he was killed in a duel at age 26. Fame first came to him with a furious foray into "political" verse. Lines from "The Death of a Poet" denounce the cold-hearted frivolity of court circles as the real cause of Pushkin's death by duel in 1837:

> You, greedy mob standing by the throne,
> Executioners of Freedom, Genius, and Glory!
> Hidden under the protection of laws,
> Before you justice and truth are silent!

A lament for Pushkin's tragic fate became a clear attack on the repression and foppery of the Nicholas era. Unpublished and passed in manuscript from hand to hand, the poem's popularity was instantaneous.

Czar Nicholas could hardly ignore such an insolent attack, especially coming from a young officer in the Hussar Guards protecting his country palace in Tsarskoye Selo. Lermontov was sent off to a quiet outpost in the Caucasus, where he wrote a number of poems published in the Petersburg press, which earned him an enormous reputation. His grandmother agitated for his return, and within a year he was back with his old regiment. But not for long. He promptly picked a duel with the son of the French ambassador. Neither was hurt, but the czar was furious. Lermontov was again exiled to the Army of the Caucasus, this time to fight fearsome mountain tribesmen.

Lermontov's commanding officers cited the disgraced youth for reckless courage in battle and recommended decorations, suggestions which were ignored in Petersburg. He finally received permission to take leave in Moscow and Petersburg at the end of 1840. On his return to the Caucasus in early 1841, he quarreled with an old schoolmate and was killed in yet another duel.

The spirit of the Caucasus breathes through both his poetry and his paintings. Views of Tbilisi, Dagestan, Pyatigorsk, and the mountains themselves are rendered with a vivid color and drama resembling that of Delacroix. Hung in elegant Moscow chambers, the paintings illustrate wonderfully the dichotomies of his life: from European drawing-room society to battles and adventures on the frontier of Europe. Like his hero Byron, Lermontov lived ruggedly among warriors and exulted in the charms of exotic women. His work has the color and grace of a fairy-tale world, as if his life served simply as the creation of a vivid, enchanting myth.

Pushkin, the Decembrist revolutionaries, and Lermontov all exhibited a slightly unreal approach to life. They lived as if their romantic conceptions of politics, love, and adventure should come true. Hereditary wealth helped to insulate them from the grimy worries of everyday life, but then they ran smack into the arch-reality of Nicholas and his persnickety police. The Nicholas Age was heaven for titled rakes and corrupt officials, but anyone with a trace of liberalism, or aspirations beyond the accumulation of lucre and tarts, was made miserable.

After the Lermontov Museum continue up **Malaya Molchanovka Street**. It was the site of a settlement for a regiment of *streltsy*, and was called Streltsy Lane until in the eighteenth century it was renamed for Mikhail Molchanov, who commanded the regiment in the defense of the Arbat Gate against the Poles in 1612. Half a block up the street we reach Rzhevsky Lane, where we will make a right and continue five blocks until we reach Herzen Street. (Rzhevsky Lane changes to Paliashvili Street after one block.) In the late eighteenth and early nineteenth

131

An art nouveau mansion designed by Solovyov

centuries this area was settled by the nobility, but not those with great wealth. The tree-lined street today shows architecture primarily from the nineteenth and early twentieth centuries.

Stop in front of the house at the far right corner of Khlebny (Bread) Lane and Paliashvili Street. (Khlebny is the second street we will cross after making our right off Malaya Molchanovka.) This building houses the Georgian Republic's permanent representative in Moscow, as noted on the plaques out front. It is worth taking a close look because the art nouveau building, designed by S. U. Solovyov in the early 1900s, shows how much Russian architecture had changed by the turn of the twentieth century.

Strange as it sounds, the international art nouveau movement allowed Russian architecture to flower again with its own strange genius, after its entry into the Western tradition. In the eighteenth and nineteenth centuries, the imported classical motifs played out over facades, while buildings remained symmetrical and surface oriented. Art nouveau changed all this with a different conception of structure: exteriors would bulge with the expression of interior layout; facades would become saturated with color and unexpected shapes. This allowed each country practicing art nouveau to draw on its particular folk and medieval art traditions to adorn buildings both inside and out.

The example in front of us is a particularly fine one. Asymmetry is evident in the two wings, the right with a peaked roof and the left flatter, set back, and crowned by wrought iron. The tilework, and brick and stone contrasts, which hearken back to fifteenth-century churches, are especially characteristic features of Russian art nouveau.

Continue down Paliashvili another three blocks until you reach the intersecting Herzen Street. The names of other intersecting lanes along the way tell the story of the area's earlier times. Vorovskogo, the first street we crossed after turning off Malaya Molchanovka, was once named Povarskaya (Cook) Street, in reference to the czar's cooks who had their settlement here from the seventeenth century. Khlebny (Bread) Lane was the settlement for royal bakers, followed by Skatertny (Tablecloth) Lane, for the workers who produced table linens for the Kremlin, and finally the Stolovy (Dining Room) Lane, for royal waiters and kitchen workers. Old Moscow was divided into neighborhoods on the basis of profession, and street names echo this bustle of the distant past.

Herzen Street, named for nineteenth-century essayist and radical Alexander Herzen, was once called Bolshaya Nikitskaya Street, and to the right toward the Kremlin is lined by grand classical mansions of the eighteenth century. One block behind us, on Stolovy Lane, the mother of Peter the Great, Natalya Naryshkin, had her palace. In 1685 she built opposite her residence the **Church of the Great Ascension**, which survived until the end of the eighteenth century, when it was replaced by the lovely and austere classical church (reconstructed 1820–31) we see now, and which has kept the old name. It is an example of pristine Russian classicism, before Renaissance-style ornament began to encrust facades. Long dilapidated and closed, the church is now under restoration.

It is here that Pushkin and Natalya Goncharova were

The Church of the Great Ascension

married in 1831. It is not far-fetched to see a parallel between Pushkin's clean and symmetrical poetic style and this architecture. Both he and the church were products of the same classical age that never let ornament overcome conception.

A very different type of life awaits us just beyond the church where Herzen Street forks into Kachalova (formerly Malaya Nikitskaya) Street. Right at the corner is one of Moscow's great architectural monuments, the **Ryabushinsky Mansion** (1900–02) by Fyodor Shekhtel, the equal of the Brussels houses of Horta and Hankar. On Walk 2, we passed the Ryabushinsky Bank, one of the sources of the merchant family's wealth.

Far from being a lifeless monument to greed, the mansion unfurls life force in full throng of color and arabesque. From the looping garden rail to the leaf-shaped window patterns to the facade mosaics to the asymmetrical and odd windows, the building shows off exuberant love of life. It is the perfect emblem of the *fin de siècle* in Russia, when merchant fortunes found worthy artists to support. It is hard to begrudge a man his wealth when he puts it to such good use.

The interior of the mansion is a dream world sustained by the best materials and design money could buy: stained glass, a marble stairway folded and twisted like flowing lava, wave lash and arabesques of mahogany, and asters blooming in plaster relief.

After the Revolution the Ryabushinsky family lost the mansion, and in the 1930s it became the residence of the great proletarian writer Maxim Gorky, raised among the laborers who later populated his plays and novels. The mansion is now the **Maksim Gorky Museum** (open Wednesday and Friday from noon to 8:00 P.M.; Thursday, Saturday, and Sunday from 10:00 A.M. to 5:45 P.M.; and closed Monday and Tuesday). Gorky's life here was sad with irony. Having spent years in Italy, ostensibly for his health, he returned at the encouragement of Stalin and worked as chairman of the Writers Union and as a mouthpiece of the regime, even while he tried to protect his colleagues from arrest. Some believe that he was eventually assassinated on Stalin's orders through the use of poisoned candy. Pictures in the museum give a good idea of the ceremonial functions he fulfilled, from meeting with peasants to ruminating with left-wing French intellectuals, to reading to Stalin and his generals. In one hundred years life had come full circle: another Russian artist was serving as window dressing to the "czar."

The physical resemblance of many of the buildings on this walk to those in Western capitals is striking. Nineteenth-century Russia built in Western style, and took pride in participating in European power politics, especially after the defeat of Napoleon. Yet we learned in the Kremlin to be suspicious of appearances: Ivan III's import of Italian architects to build Russia's most important cathedrals changed the look of Moscow without necessarily altering its essence. Moscow's Empire mansions look as though they were built for glittering salons to rival those of Paris, and indeed they often were and did. By the nineteenth century, Russia had fully entered the mainstream of European culture, and by the twentieth, she was vying with France and England for leadership in music, painting, and poetry.

Yet Russia remained an autocracy. Informers stalked the elegant parquet, eavesdropping on idle chitchat and the seditious talk of acquaintances. There was an atmosphere of mutual suspicion, which has begun to break down only in the last decade of Romanov rule. It was difficult to lead a life free of political considerations unless you were a dunderhead of large proportions. The shadow of the czar fell on innocent exchanges, simply out of fear that any subject could turn into an enemy of the throne.

The natural fear of the autocrat, who must sense the fraudulence of his claim to power, engendered an underlying sense of insecurity in the society as a whole. Despite Russia's magnificent absorption and adaptation of western culture, European neighbors looked askance at its political institutions, and even questioned the virtue of its art. "These apprentices of fashion are trained bears, the sight of which inclines me to regret the wild ones," was the stinging remark of the French Marquis de Custine. Russians were deeply offended by such observations, but their discomfort is perhaps one source of the great psychological novels and plays, which could hardly have been produced in an environment of complacency and self-satisfaction. Russia's autocracy has led to refined estimates of moral culpability, and a powerful desire to reform.

LENINGRAD
WALKS

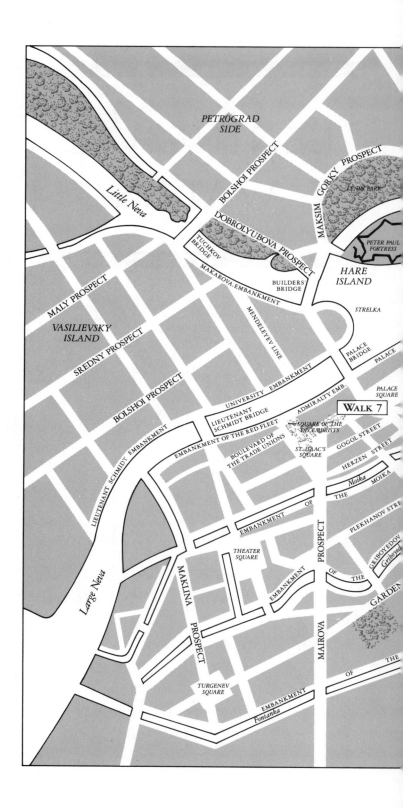

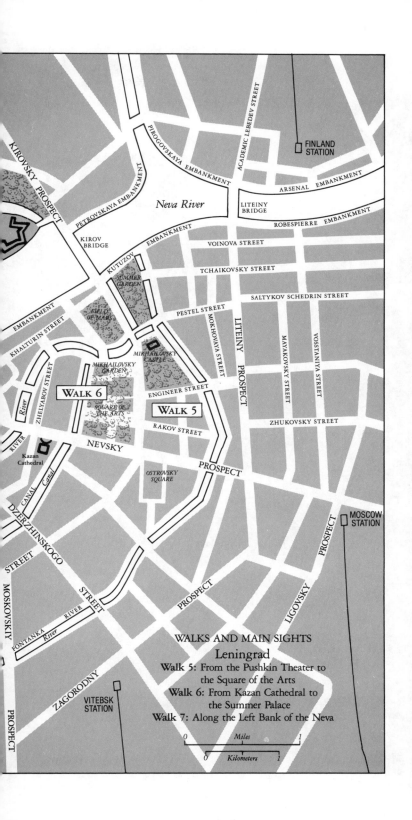

WALKS AND MAIN SIGHTS
Leningrad
Walk 5: From the Pushkin Theater to
the Square of the Arts
Walk 6: From Kazan Cathedral to
the Summer Palace
Walk 7: Along the Left Bank of the Neva

0   Miles   1

0   Kilometers   1

Walk · 5

From the Pushkin Theater to the Square of the Arts

Entry gate to the Sheremetyev Palace

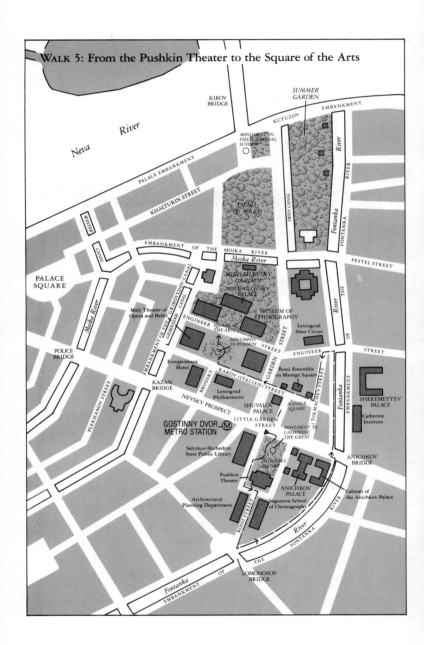

WALK 5: From the Pushkin Theater to the Square of the Arts

Neva River

KIROV BRIDGE

SUMMER GARDEN

KUTUZOV

EMBANKMENT

MONUMENT TO FIELD-MARSHAL SUVOROV

PALACE EMBANKMENT

SWAN CANAL

Fontanka River

KHALTURIN STREET

WINTER CANAL

FIELD OF MARS

PALACE SQUARE

EMBANKMENT OF THE MOIKA RIVER

Moika River

PESTEL STREET

MIKHAILOVSKY GARDEN

EMBANKMENT OF THE GRIBOYEDOV CANAL

MIKHAILOVSKY PALACE

Moika River

Maly Theater of Opera and Ballet

ENGINEER SQUARE OF THE ARTS

MUSEUM OF ETHNOGRAPHY

GARDEN STREET

Leningrad State Circus

POLICE BRIDGE

MONUMENT TO PUSHKIN

ENGINEER STREET

THE FONTANKA RIVER

Evropeiskaya Hotel

Rossi Ensemble on Manege Square

SHEREMETYEV PALACE

KAZAN BRIDGE

BRODSKY

RAKOV (ITALIAN) STREET

Leningrad Philharmonic

SHUVALOV PALACE

MANEGE SQUARE

TOLMACHEV STREET

FONTANKA EMBANKMENT

Catherine Institute

PLEKHANOV STREET

NEVSKY PROSPECT

LITTLE GARDEN STREET

GOSTINNY DVOR (M) METRO STATION

Saltykov-Shchedrin State Public Library

MONUMENT TO CATHERINE THE GREAT

ANICHKOV BRIDGE

Pushkin Theater

(OSTROVSKY) SQUARE

ANICHKOV PALACE

Cabinet of the Anichkov Palace

Architectural Planning Department

ROSSI STREET

Vaganova School of Choreography

THE FONTANKA RIVER

Fontanka EMBANKMENT OF THE

LOMONOSOV BRIDGE

Starting Point: At Ostrovsky Square, next to Gostinniy Dvor (Shopping Arcade)
Walk Length: 2 hours
Metro Stop: Gostinniy Dvor. This metro has three exits. Take either one of the two leading to Gostinniy Dvor itself (the third leads to the Griboyedov Canal). In both cases Ostrovsky Square is to the left as you face Gostinniy Dvor.

Immediately to the right of the Public Library and Ostrovsky Square is Gostinniy Dvor (the Shopping Arcade), dating from the eighteenth century and still housing a variety of stores. You might want to try browsing there.

This is an ideal walk to combine with a visit to the Russian Museum of Art (Mikhailovsky Palace), which is our last stop. The walk could be done in the morning, followed by lunch and the museum. Except for Tuesday, it is open daily from 10:00 A.M. to 6:15 P.M. (last entry at 5:15), and on Thursdays from 10:00 A.M. until 8:15 P.M. (last entry at 7:15). The museum cafeteria serves coffee, wine, cognac, pastries, and open face sandwiches. Its hours are 11:00 A.M. until 4:00 P.M. daily, except for Monday when it closes an hour early. There is a break every day from 2:00 until 2:15. If you prefer something more substantial, try one of the restaurants we have listed on nearby Nevsky Prospect.

It is tempting to begin a tour of Leningrad with views of the vast Neva River and its grand palaces, of the Senate

Square where the *Bronze Horseman* rides and the Decembrists revolted for democracy in 1825, and of the Admiralty whose golden spire marks the center of the city.
A march along the left bank of the Neva is like an introduction to Paris by the Seine. The river mirrors the city
at its most regal and dazzling, but such a walk holds the
danger of overwhelming the first-time visitor. Leningrad
can be so extraordinary that it is difficult afterward to
recall the details of its loveliness, the reason for its powerful effect. The tourist returns home full of praises that
leave neighbor and friend bewildered. Perhaps this is one
reason the city is so little known and its beauty unfabled.
Leningrad has its partisans who regard it as the most
beautiful city in Europe. We plan to send you home fully
able to explain why.

Toward that end we ignore for now the beckoning
Neva and concentrate instead on inland blocks that pos-
sess a quieter beauty. Here, the danger of being stunned
is less. The city simply accumulates facade by colonnaded facade, vista by vista beneath the streaking sky,
and winding canal by lamplit footbridge, until its logic
carves a permanent place in the heart. Leningrad has few
individually great buildings (by this standard Moscow
stands far above); it is a city of ensembles. The individual
facade exists not for itself but as part of a larger plan.
Lovers of Gothic mysticism in architecture should come
here before they denounce the possibilities that lie in
baroque and classical design. Facades, squares, and streets
perfect in proportion have endlessly been laid, and endlessly been broken by wandering canals and the Neva
itself, by even the trees in the city's many careful parks
and gardens.

The architectural rules of the Enlightenment reign supreme, almost without the interruption of Romanesque,
Gothic, or modern buildings as in other European cities,
which might undermine the dream of geometry and ideal
orders. After Paris's Notre Dame, St. Sulpice is cold and
heartless. Leningrad has no Notre Dame; it is a classical

despotism, Plato's vision of *polis* realized without the challenge of other ages. Here we can forget the Gothic of both West and East, the urgent medieval seeking after God. A ladder of civil-service grades divided the lowest ink-stained clerk from the counselor to the czar. No chasm lay between them, only an incremental series of ranks; both clerk and statesman were part of the same cosmos ruled over by the czar. Leningrad is a city of ranks, of palaces built in scale to authority, and of public monuments and churches built in praise of the state.

We begin with Leningrad's most perfect architect of proportion, Carlo Rossi (1775–1849), the son of a successful Italian ballerina who made her career in Petersburg. His buildings and plazas read like stage sets on which life could unfold in magnificent surroundings. That is, we begin on Nevsky Prospect, staring through a park at the **Pushkin** (formerly Alexandrinsky) **Theater** (1828–32), more noble for its distance from us. The building is only slightly wider than the park's major path bordered by trees. This is what is meant by the word *vista*, at least in Leningrad. Lines of sight are channeled directly toward specific facades, in this case a loggia of white columns framed by yellow masonry with white Empire detailing. A bronze-charioted Apollo rides the cornice, and in classic Empire style the building is crowned by a stepped-back pointed roof.

Before you enter the park, look to your right down Nevsky Prospect. In a muted glowing (or if the sun is out, glistening) at the distant end is the gilded spire of the **Admiralty**, mounted on an Empire pavilion of white columns. Here is yet another vista. The three major avenues on this side of the Neva converge on the Admiralty like radii on the center of a semicircle. Its needlelike spire is the compass point of the city, and its facade seems to turn all ways, serving as grand end to the vistas of all three avenues (Nevsky, Dzerzhinskogo, and Maiorova). Leningrad's plan is a sublime sort of geometry, drawn not in harsh lines but with boundaries marked by columns and pilasters.

There remains the as yet unexplained word *ensemble*, which is equally key to understanding Leningrad. Think of Nevsky Prospect as one giant vista leading to the Admiralty. Intersecting at the perpendicular are a series of smaller vistas, each with its own harmonic ensemble around the central building, as is the case here around the Pushkin Theater. These ensembles are like pauses, or even deep breaths, taken on a straight and narrow journey.

Ostrovsky Square opens off Nevsky like a mechanical lung filling itself with air. The Pushkin Theater and the other buildings surrounding are an example of soothing arrangement—ensemble. Each amplifies the other. On the right is the **State Public Library** (the second largest in the Soviet Union), built in 1796–1801 by E. Sokolov. Rossi added the major portion of the library that faces the square in 1828–32, the same years that he built the Alexandrinsky (now Pushkin) Theater. The library is far from a mirror of the theater: it uses Ionic (as opposed to Corinthian) orders, a shallower portico, and differently arranged windows, but even these distinctions make clear the buildings' similarity in spirit. Lest we forget that classicism is more than simply proportion and Greek capitals, Rossi adorns this building also with sculptures appropriate to its function: from left to right Herodotus, Cicero, Tacitus, Virgil, Demosthenes, Hippocrates, Euripides, Euclid, Plato, and Homer, with Minerva, the goddess of wisdom, crowning the facade.

On most days an informal bazaar is underway along the Ostrovsky Square gates facing the library, and old-seeming icons are particularly in evidence. Don't believe the dates quoted by the salesmen and don't use dollars, but you may find something you like.

On the other side of Ostrovsky Square (opposite the library and across the street) are two separate pavilions

(1816–18) by Rossi, now part of the Anichkov Palace Garden to the left. Along with the wrought-iron fence, the two pavilions are Rossi's earliest works. From the dates (1816 for the start of the pavilions and 1834 for the completion of the surrounding streets) we can say that the entire ensemble took eighteen years to build. Often, especially when more than one architect was involved, such arrangements took decades. This is especially the case with ensembles that include baroque buildings (dating up to the early 1760s), which were often conceived to stand alone. It was beginning with Catherine the Great's reign (1762–96) that architects evinced such an obsession with harmonic groupings.

Directly across Nevsky Prospect from the pavilion on the corner is **Gastronom #1** (formerly Yeliseyev's Food Emporium), built in 1902–03 in early art nouveau style, an exception to Leningrad's architectural homogeneity. Its interior fixtures are intact and give some idea of the opulence in which Petersburg's prosperous shopped for delicacies from across Europe and Asia in pre-Revolutionary days.

Now enter Ostrovsky Square itself. In the center is a huge **monument to Catherine the Great**, (1873) with her favorites on the pedestal at her feet. Marshal Grigori Potemkin is at the front center stepping on a turban, to signify victories over the Turks won in the Black Sea area. The lovely woman with flowing hair and an open book is the Countess Dashkova, who at nineteen helped intrigue to fell Peter III (who wanted to marry her sister) and put Catherine on the throne. In real life she was more homely than suggested here, or as Catherine wickedly remarked, "she was far prettier than her sister who was very ugly." Other figures include Field Marshals Suvorov and Rumyantsev (on either side of Potemkin); the great court poet Gavril Derzhavin (next to Dashkova); and Catherine's first great lover, the Guards officer Aleksei Orlov, who was central in the coup that put her on the throne.

Approach the theater itself (you'll notice more out-

View down Rossi Street to Pushkin Theater

door market stalls on that side of the square as well), and walk to the right, circling around it to the other side. Another architectural lesson is in store. Leningrad's great Empire buildings face two ways—they serve two vistas. With your back to the theater, you look down Rossi (formerly Theater) Street, now named for the architect. Perfect symmetry rules: the street is 22 meters (about 24 yards) across, identical to the height of the two long columned buildings, which stretch to a length ten times their height, 220 meters (about 240 yards). Even more perfect is the view back toward the theater from farther down the street. Here the stage-managed vista takes its most perfect expression. On your right **(#2/6 Rossi Street)** is the Museum of Russian and Soviet Theater as well as the renowned Vaganova School of Choreography, while the opposite enfilade **(#1/3 Rossi Street)** was the Ministry of Education until the Revolution, and is now the Main Architectural Planning Department for the city.

Rossi Street enters a traffic circle on the Fontanka River, which is where this ensemble ends after stretching from Nevsky Prospect to the granite **Lomonosov** (formerly Chernyshov) **Bridge**. Rossi also did the curving buildings to the right, which echo the arc of the circle.

148

Think of ensembles not in terms of individual buildings but as arrangements bringing order to whole sectors of the city. In the course of this walk you should grow no more tired of subtly varying columns than of commas in prose. As important as the buildings themselves is the geometric order they imply. Leningrad is a city of pristine logic that has room for the changing color of the sky and the irregular silver mirror of water.

The Lomonosov Bridge was built in 1785–87, one of seven identical structures built over the Fontanka River in Catherine II's reign (only one other survives). It used to be a drawbridge and the chains that lifted the middle section are still visible. The granite form is strange and original, its weighty gray pavilions an adaptation in miniature form from classical structures. Leningrad architects were already assimilating, as opposed to simply copying, the Western architectural language.

Staying on this side of the Fontanka, walk to your left back toward Nevsky Prospect and the bronze-horse trammeled **Anichkov Bridge**. It was first built across the river in wood in 1715, and reconstructed many times until it reached its current form in 1841, when it was decorated with the equestrian sculptures by P. K. Klodt.

The river marked the boundary of the city until the beginning of the nineteenth century, and many nobles had their country mansions with huge gardens here on the embankment, which was also a convenient site for hunting game. The name Fontanka comes from the Russian word for "fountain," because the river fed the fountains in Peter the Great's Summer Garden farther up the river. Many estates along the river had the advantage of natural springs, which eliminated the need for digging wells.

On your left, the two-story building with a colonnaded central entrance on the corner of Nevsky Prospect and the Fontanka is the **Cabinet** of the Anichkov Palace, built in 1803–05 by Giacomo Quarenghi. The **Anichkov Palace** (1741–54) itself, the oldest building on Nevsky Prospect, is hidden behind the nineteenth-century Cabi-

The Lomonosov Bridge

net. You can see the side of the older baroque palace from Nevsky Prospect, but its main facade was meant to front the Fontanka. Originally, a canal coming off the river led right up to the steps of the palace, which could be approached by boat. Its annexes, gardens, and orchards covered the territory that is now occupied by the Pushkin Theater, Ostrovsky Square, and Public Library, all the way to the Lomonosov Bridge. Incidentally, the architect, Zemtsov, was one of the first Russians to design and build Western-style buildings in Petersburg. Until then, Peter the Great and his successors had largely relied on foreigners to design the city. Zemtsov was one of the first architectural students sent abroad on orders of Peter, to prepare for commissions at home.

The Anichkov Palace was reconstructed in 1778–79 so that its exterior has a fully classical appearance. The self-enclosed layout, however, is a good illustration of the difference between baroque and classical planning. Even with their grand views, baroque palaces were conceived as regal entities unto themselves, rather than in relation to other buildings.

The luxury-loving Empress Elizabeth (reigned 1741–61) commissioned this building (along with many others including the Winter Palace), and made a present of it to her lover, Count Alexei Razumovsky, a simple uneducated Cossack who won her heart and his title with a magnificent singing voice. He was the most important man in the empire for the duration of her reign, and delighted in beating better-born nobles when he was drunk.

Elizabeth loved to eat, tipple, and visit the theater, where performances began after 11:00 P.M. so as to accommodate her schedule. She rarely retired before 5:00 A.M. and spent most of the day in bed, when carriages and sometimes foot traffic were forbidden in nearby streets so as not to rouse her from peaceful slumber. For that matter, the rest of the nobility was probably in bed, too; Elizabeth required their presence at the late-night theater on threat of heavy fines. Her passion for dresses, jewelry, and buildings left the treasury bankrupt by the time of her death. However, she did earn some affection from the public for outlawing capital punishment entirely and for her conscientious religious observance.

Yet the portrait Catherine II draws of her in her memoirs is far from that of a bon vivant. Under Elizabeth the court was riddled with informers reporting not only on the entourage but on the royal family itself. Catherine's child, Paul, was removed from her custody and raised separately; he grew up to hate his mother. Nobles, officers, and civil servants alike were casually ruined and exiled to Siberia, a practice which even ruthless Catherine denounced as gratuitous. By the way, Catherine in her turn gave the Anichkov Palace to her favorite, Grigori Potemkin.

Where Nevsky Prospect crosses the Anichkov Bridge, guards were stationed to check the passports and documents of people entering the city, as was the case on every road leading into the forest. The barrier went up at 11:00 P.M. and was not opened until dawn. Only nobles, priests, doctors, midwives, officials, and people with special permission were permitted to pass, and then only when they were carrying lanterns. Even the aristocracy was subject to this rule, just as they were subject to the denunciations of informers. Perhaps there was a legitimate security reason for this care. The forests on the far side of the Fontanka hid robbers eager to pounce on travelers.

Sculpture on the Anichkov Bridge

Before we continue, take note of the spectacular red palace, at **#41 Nevsky**, across the river on the right-hand corner of the bridge. Although it looks like a perfect example of mid-eighteenth century architecture, it in fact dates from 1848, when A. Stackensneider built it for Prince Beloselsky-Belozersky, a highly literate man who translated many Russian classics into French. It is strange to think that the *Communist Manifesto* was completed the same year as the building.

Immediately to the right of the **Beloselsky-Belozersky Palace** (as we face it), at **#46 Fontanka**, is a red palace with cream details and a green roof. The original structure is very early (dating from the first half of the eighteenth century), but it was rebuilt in 1843 in an even more decorative neo-baroque style. Note the fabulous iron gate to the left, and the flanking wall topped by additional ironwork. As you walk through the city, be alert not only

The Beloselsky-Belozersky Palace

to vistas and the symmetry of ensembles but to luxurious ironwork as well, from mansion and garden railings to the lanterns dangling from bridges.

Now cross Nevksy Prospect and continue along this side of the Fontanka embankment. Shortly after the intersection are granite steps leading from the sidewalk down to a dock. **Boat tours of the Fontanka** depart from here every 15 to 30 minutes in the summer, and every hour in the ice-free parts of fall and spring. Fare is 80 kopecks for the standard 45-minute tour (a 90-minute tour is sometimes also available). If you have the time, the trip is worth taking. The ticket kiosk is on the embankment just beyond the steps.

On the left (#21) is the olive-beige **Shuvalov Palace**, with a distinct bay window interrupting the normal course of pilasters and an ornate frieze with cupids stretching just below the cornice. It was built around 1800 and then reconstructed in 1844–46 in Italian Renaissance style, when the Shuvalovs (an old noble family) bought it to add to another family palace a few blocks away, which we will soon see.

Continue along the embankment past the first intersection on the left at Rakov Street (Ulitsa Rakova), formerly Italian Street (Italianskaya Ulitsa). Directly across the river from the intersection is a massive building (**#36 Fontanka**) in pure classical style with an array of repeating columns. It was built as a prestigious girls' school, the Catherine Institute, in 1804–07 by Quarenghi (who did the Anichkov Palace Cabinet we saw earlier), and now serves as an extension to the Public Library. Faithful to the canons of city planning, the building plays an important role that is not evident from here. Its central portico completes the Rakov Street vista in the same way the Pushkin Theater completes Rossi Street. Later in the walk we get the view down the length of Rakov Street, which seems from a distance to leap the river and touch the columned entrance.

One of the jewels of the Fontanka is immediately to the left of the Catherine Institute: the **Sheremetyev Palace** at Fontanka #34. It started out at the end of the 1730s as a single-story stone building and was reconstructed in 1750–55 by architect Savva Chevakinsky into the grandiose monument we see today. In the mid-eighteenth century it was considered a country palace. The decorative grille and gates, with the gilded Sheremetyev coat of arms above the entrance, were designed by I. Corsini in 1837–38.

The Sheremetyev family was especially powerful in Peter the Great's time, when Boris Sheremetyev served as a top general and field marshal. Catherine I is said to have passed through his bed as mistress before she was taken up by Peter. When later she married, and then finally succeeded the czar, European courts were charmed by the fact that the illiterate empress of Russia, once an orphan servant girl, carefully deferred to royalty of more exalted lineage.

One must always be careful not to confuse this Catherine with Catherine II (the Great), originally a German princess, who was so far from illiterate that she corresponded with the French *philosophes*. They did wonders for her public image in the West, the same way Sartre and other French leftists would perfume Stalinism over 150 years later.

The building has taken on a very different sort of life this century in the poetry of Anna Akhmatova, who lived in a wing of the palace overlooking the rear courtyard:

> I make no claim
> On this illustrious house,
> But it has turned out that almost all my life
> I have spent under the notable roof
> Of the Fontanka Palace . . . I destitute
> Came and destitute leave . . .

Once lighted with the glitter of balls, the grand palace became counterpoint to Akhmatova's desperate existence and fear of arrest. Her apartment is now a museum open from 10:30 A.M. to 6:30 P.M. (last entry at 5:30) every day except Monday and the final Wednesday of each month. To get there, enter the front gate of the palace, walk through the archway on the left, and follow the arrows. The museum entrance is on the opposite side of the rear garden courtyard. If you want a closer look at the palace, cross over at Belinsky Bridge just ahead.

Also across the bridge is the early **Church of Saints Simon and Anna** (1731–34), which was built by Zemtsov, original designer of the Anichkov Palace. This is the only building of his which survives intact. It is close in style to the Moscow Baroque churches of the older capital, with a startling difference: the belltower is peaked by a ribbed spire rather than a ribbed cupola. The spire could have crowned a church in a town in Sweden or the Hanseatic League, and it is one of the motifs of Petersburg architecture, from the Admiralty to the Mikhailovsky Castle.

On this side of the bridge we stand in Belinsky Square. Diagonally across from us the building with three windowed archways above three entrances is the **Leningrad State Circus** (Fontanka #3). It was built in 1876–

77 on orders of Italian impresario Giacomo Ciniselli, and served as the first permanent circus building in Russia, which had long known traveling troupes. In the past 100 years Russia has probably produced more great clowns than any other country in the world. You might consider going. A museum of circus history in the building is open noon to 5:00 P.M. every day except Sunday.

You should now follow a course back the way we came, only on Tolmachev Street (Ulitsa Tolmacheva), which is sharply to the left with your back to the river. Notice the wrought-iron balconies at #8. After one block we reach the Manezh Square (Manezhnaya Ploshad'), with Rakov Street (Ulitsa Rakova) running the length of the square on the far side.

Hard on the right at **#6 Manezh Square** is a compact classical building that was rebuilt by Carlo Rossi in 1823–24. Yellow with white detailing and two massive columns, it is terse and elegant. Two buildings farther down is a much larger building, the **Winter Manezh**, also rebuilt by Rossi in 1823–24. Then comes a garden with a high back wall topped by a grille and urns silhouetted against the sky. Finally, at the end of the garden is a pavilion duplicating the first one. The three buildings work together to define this square. You can better take in the beauty of the arrangement by standing back. The large building between the first and second Rossi works shouldn't be there; we suspect the space was taken up by a second garden.

It is time to look back toward the Fontanka from Rakov Street (and not from deep in Manezh Square, which borders it). There it is: another vista, this time leading to the **Catherine Institute**, which we saw when we walked along the Fontanka Embankment. Vistas somehow shorten the distance between two points. They link up various sectors of the city. By virtue of the Catherine Institute, this square is tied to the Fontanka.

Now recall the very beginning of the walk and the first vista we saw—of Rossi's Pushkin Theater. Then walk down Rakov Street to the corner of Little Garden (Malaya Sadovaya) Street, the next intersection, and look to the left. There it is again—the facade of the Pushkin Theater. You can wander a circuitous course for an hour and a half and still not escape the grid. There is something relentless in this conception. Be thankful for the street life, the noise, and the trees. As you walk you should begin to feel all sorts of rhythms: the columns and pilasters of a facade, and the subtle shift to another palace; the sudden opening to the side of a new ensemble; and the approaching portico of the "temple" at the end of a vista.

Rakov was formerly Italian Street (Italianskaya Ulitsa), named perhaps out of gratitude for Italianate experiments in perspective. You will notice large white plaques, elegantly typeset, mounted on many buildings as you walk down this street and others in the city center. These are the old street names. Many local residents are in a hurry to dispense with the current names and return to the glories of old St. Petersburg. In this instance, the street is named for a Commissar Rakov, who died in 1919 in the defense of the city approaches from White Army attack.

Across Malaya Sadovaya on the left (25 Rakov Street) is a blue building with white detailing, the **Shuvalov Palace** (1753–55) by Chevakinsky (the architect of the Sheremetyev Palace on the Fontanka). The whole block it occupies back to Nevsky Prospect was once part of the Shuvalov estate. In the eighteenth century, such baroque palaces grandly overlooked gardens, orchards, and vegetable plots. The Shuvalov family was one of the leading clans in Russia, and many an emperor or empress accepted the invitation to dine here. This did not protect Count Ivan Shuvalov from beatings at the hands of Empress Elizabeth's favorite, the strapping Cossack with a beautiful voice, Alexei Razumovsky (perhaps because Shuvalov himself had once been a lover of Elizabeth's). In fact, Countess Shuvalova arranged special religious services every time her husband was required to hunt with the First Lover—to protect him from much-feared blows of the cudgel.

President of the Academy of the Arts and a patron of literature and painting in his own right, Shuvalov turned his residence into an intellectuals' salon. Among his frequent guests was Mikhail Lomonosov, a legendary figure in Russian scientific and literary history. The son of a fisherman, Lomonosov ran away from home at age 12 to get an education. He evolved into one of the greatest physicists and chemists of the eighteenth century, was the major poet of his generation, and founded both modern Russian (through his poetry and grammatical textbooks) and Moscow University. Mathematics, mining, mosaics, and history were other subjects that he showed an extraordinary talent for, but he did have his quirks, including drink and a touchy personality.

One man Lomonosov loathed was Alexander Sumarokov, a talented gentleman-poet, playwright, and rival for literary fame, also a frequent visitor at the Shuvalovs. "In arguments, the angrier Sumarokov got, the more sarcastic toward him Lomonosov became," Shuvalov once described. "If both weren't completely sober, the argument ended in such furious swearing that I was compelled to kick them both out."

However, Shuvalov and his friends were not above setting the two at each other for entertainment. When Lomonosov got carried away on the subject of Sumarokov, Shuvalov would send for the target of the abuse, and then carefully keep Lomonosov on the subject. When Sumarokov arrived and heard the voice of his enemy, he would either abruptly leave or storm in shouting:

"Don't believe him, Your Excellency, everything he says is a lie; I am amazed that you allow a place in your home to such a drunken scoundrel!"

"You are a drunkard yourself," Lomonosov once answered furiously, "an ignoramus who got his education under the floor of a schoolhouse, and all your plays are stolen!"

159

Petersburg's stately facades hid a great deal of passion. Stage set is the best metaphor for the city. It is no wonder that the theatrical arts have for over two centuries remained at such a high level. Think of the Kirov Ballet today. The city incites the grand gesture with its regal backdrops, and inspires delusions of perfect order with its harmony. Only in art, perhaps only on the stage, can the grandeur and artificial order the city seeks be realized. Leningrad is a city that tolerates the teeming life of millions of residents on its plazas and avenues, but their irregular gait, unfinished business, and longing does not touch the architecture. It stands arrogantly aloof, the haven of czars and nobles who needed to fool their subjects with dignified exteriors.

Yet there are gradations of rank in these facades. The whole city is one of order, and every citizen participates with some particular and assigned rank. Peter the Great commissioned architects to design model residences for grandees, nobles, merchants, and the poor. These models were implemented by law, and expensive stone construction was required of the upper classes, who moved unwillingly to the city when it was still a swamp. The city is an artificial creation, Peter's dream risen up out of the black North. Like Venice, the very unlikeliness of its site makes it more startling and strange, especially during seasonal extremes, like the White Nights of the summer solstice.

We speak of rank because of the ensemble that concludes this walk. In this city of ensembles, not all are of equal status. The **Square of the Arts** (Ploshad' Iskusstva) opens up one block farther on, a monumental arrangement following the more intimate Manezh Square we have just left. Crowning the Square of the Arts to the right (as we enter it) is Rossi's **Mikhailovsky Palace** (1819–25), which is now the Russian Museum. The palace was built and named for the Grand Duke Mikhail, and completed the year his brother, Nicholas I, ascended the throne amid the violence of the Decembrist Revolt. In style it is similar

The Mikhailovsky Palace and the monument to Pushkin on the Square of the Arts

to Rossi's other buildings, but notice how much more magnificent it is in scale.

The French Marquis de Custine was overawed by a ball held in the palace in 1839, despite his derision of so much else that was Russian: "At one of the extremities of the hall, amid thickets of exotic shrubs, a fountain threw up a column of fresh and sparkling water; its spray, illumined by innumerable wax lights, shone like the dust of diamonds and refreshed the air, always kept in agitation by the movement of the dance. It seemed like the palace of the fairies: all ideas of limits disappeared, and nothing met the eye but space, light, gold, flowers reflection, illusion, and the giddy movement of the crowd."

The reverse side of the palace overlooks the **Mikhailovsky Garden** (which we pass through on Walk 6), so that the building is incorporated into landscape as well as cityscape. On the night the French Marquis was there, the garden portico was festooned with dozens of inventive Japanese lanterns, casting shadows and lights across the palace lawns.

Rossi took good care to ensure that the square in front of the building would remain congenial by designing facades that would be required of any structure raised here in the future. Architects have faithfully followed his

161

prescriptions into the twentieth century. For example, the large building to the right of the Mikhailovsky Palace was raised in 1900–11, but harmonizes so well that it looks like a wing. It was built as the **Museum of Ethnography**. Hours are 10:00 A.M. until 6:00 P.M. daily (last entry at 5:00) except Monday and the last Friday of each month.

Overlooking the Square of the Arts to the left (as we face the palace) is the **Maly Theater of Opera and Ballet** (formerly Mikhailovsky Theater), built by A. Bryullov from 1831 to 1833. It, too, uses the facade designs provided by Rossi, as do the buildings directly across from it, and the **Leningrad Philharmonic in the name of Shostakovich** (opposite the palace) at #2/9. You might want to check what is playing in both halls, and if you see something of interest buy tickets at the box office.

The large dramatic sculpture of Pushkin reading is a recent creation by Mikhail Aniushkin. Commissioned to celebrate Leningrad's 250th birthday, it was installed in 1957.

In conceiving this massive arrangement, Rossi also cut a new street through to Nevsky Prospect. Brodsky (formerly Mikhailovsky) Street was also subjected to the architect's restrictions on facades, and where it reaches Nevsky Prospect it concludes in a small **Empire Pavilion** (now virtually a traffic island), designed clearly as an echo of the Mikhailovsky Palace portico.

Today, traffic and misguided buildings sometimes intrude upon Leningrad's underlying scheme. Caught up in the hurly-burly of the now, it is possible to lose sight of the old capital's aristocratic demeanor and order. When that happens, it is time to retire to a park bench or a café where rest will dissolve the stone and asphalt trivialities of the recent past. Leningrad's aesthetic logic remains intact and vivid to the observant walker because architects like Carlo Rossi had power. But credit also goes to Russia's restorers and conservators. After the three-year siege of the city by the Germans during World War II, many important buildings were left severely damaged. They have been painstakingly and accurately rebuilt, a symbol of love for the past despite the obscuring veil of ideology. It is revealing that today almost all political groups, from conservative communists to radical democrats, vie to portray themselves as the most committed preservationists.

Walk · 6

From Kazan
Cathedral to
the Summer Palace

A window of the Summer Palace

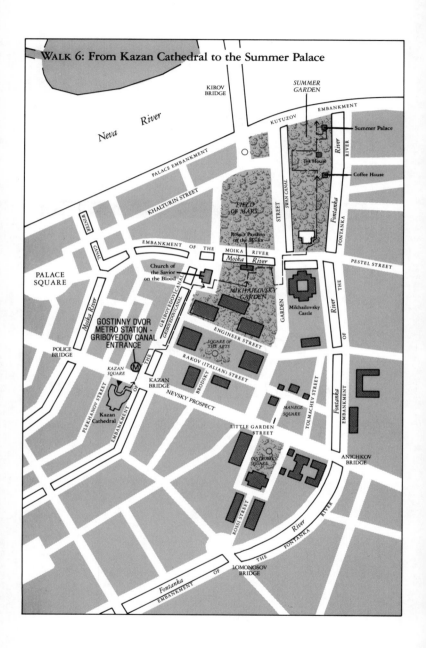

WALK 6: From Kazan Cathedral to the Summer Palace

Starting Point: At entrance to Kazan Cathedral
Walk Length: 2¹/₂ hours
Metro Stop: Gostinniy Dvor (Griboyedov Canal entrance). Exit on Nevsky Prospect, almost directly across from the cathedral.

The Kazan Cathedral has long housed the Museum of Atheism, but has recently hosted religious services attended by many officials, including Boris Yeltsin. Precise plans for the cathedral remain unclear.

The Summer Palace, which concludes this walk, is open only May through November. Its hours are noon until 8:00 P.M. except for Tuesdays when it is closed.

St. Petersburg is not merely a city of ensembles, vistas, and winding waterways. It is also a northern haven of parks and formal gardens. For another half-day we suggest resisting the temptation of the Neva River to explore nature in a classical setting. No wolves or bears pace these pathways, although well into the eighteenth century they were known within the city limits. Petersburg's parks are not nature unfurled, but tamed under the regime of architects and gardeners. Like a circus bear, the city's greenery is kept in bounds for the entertainment of residents. What is lovely is the sudden transition from streets to parks so well screened that the nearest town seems far away.

Petersburg is omnivorous. Nothing disrupts its classical

scheme—not swamps which were drained, nor streams which were widened and lined, nor trees which Peter I preserved from poaching on penalty of death. Even buildings that upset or alter classical values are somehow co-opted. On this walk we recognize the unity of Petersburg whether we are standing on a trafficked plaza or in a quiet grove.

We begin very much in the urban city, at the **Kazan Cathedral** (Kazansky Sobor), which embraces one of Nevsky Prospect's most grandiose squares. The cathedral (1801–11) is now so much of a landmark that it seems part of Petersburg's essence. Yet in 1801 the massive colonnade, copied from St. Peter's in Rome, was without precedent in Russia. Considering that the church was built to house one of Russia's most famous icons, the *Virgin of Kazan*, it is strange that the Pope's cathedral served as model.

The commissioning of the church was very much an expression of the reign of Emperor Paul I (1796–1801), who lived in the shadow of his hated mother, Catherine the Great, even after her death. Crowned at the age of forty-two, he undid as many of her policies as he could, until he fell in a coup backed by his son. Italian architecture had made a huge impression on him during his travels abroad as he waited impatiently for the throne, and one of the few positive achievements of his reign was the decision to build this cathedral.

Paul first made clear that Bernini's colonnade for St. Peter's would have to be incorporated, and then ordered a contest among the major architects of the day. The design problem was clear: religious dogma dictated that the church be oriented west-east, meaning that neither main entrance nor apse would face the prospect. What then was to be done with the colonnade? An architect came up with a plan in which a colonnade fronted the main entrance (to the right as we face the cathedral from Nevsky Prospect). Paul chose this plan, but then with the unpredictability that marked his entire reign, he changed his mind. The commission fell to Andrei Voronikhin, an almost unknown Russian.

In retrospect we can say that Voronikhin's solution was better: with a stage trickery that Carlo Rossi no doubt appreciated, he simply moved the colonnade to face Nevsky Prospect. It is almost a blind, celebrating the "wrong" entrance to the church, so as to uphold the symmetrical laws that make St. Petersburg a great city. His creation is magnificent and imposing, with a trace of sham.

Voronikhin's competitors gossiped that he had got the commission through the intervention of the powerful Count Stroganov, rumored to be his illegitimate father. Voronikhin was born a serf of the Stroganovs and won his freedom only at the age of twenty-seven, which makes his career (culminating with the prestigious title of Professor of Architecture) all the more striking. His enemies referred to him pleasantly as *rab* (slave). Even so, a self-portrait of Voronikhin reveals an intelligent and sensitive face without bitterness.

Cross Nevsky Prospect through the underpass. It will bring you up to the corner of the square, not far from the arms of looming granite. A series of older baroque churches occupied the square until the decision to build Voronikhin's monument. The older churches also housed the much revered *Virgin of Kazan*, which was said to have miraculously appeared after the fall of Kazan to Ivan the Terrible in 1579. In 1612 the icon led Russian forces to victory over Polish occupiers, further proof of its great holiness.

Yet, already in the eighteenth century modernity began to dull the icon's power. Peter the Great's founding of Petersburg was unpopular with all classes, from the poor who died driving piles in the swamp to nobles forced to build expensive palaces in a cold and wet nowhere. In 1720 the *Virgin of Kazan* began weeping. Countless parishioners saw the miracle for themselves, and the word bruited through hovel and palace alike: the Virgin was dissatisfied with both the new capital and the anti-Christian czar. Peter's mockery of Church traditions and his devotion to all things Western was dry tinder to the incendiary divine. A more superstitious man would have begun to doubt himself, but Peter believed in the machinery of the West. He rushed back from travel in the north and stormed into the cathedral. The icon was removed from its mount and a chamber of viscous oil revealed. With the heat of dozens of supplicant candles, the oil had slowly dripped through pinprick holes in the Virgin's eyes. "I order that from now on Virgins not cry," Peter announced in a public *prikaz*, "and if a Virgin once cries with oil, then the priests will cry blood."

Walk right up to the central portico and take a look at the bronze doors. They are a copy of Lorenzo Ghiberti's bronze doors for the Baptistry in Florence, based on a plaster cast. Thread your way through the columns for a few minutes to get a feel for the weight of the whole structure. This is one of the few places in Petersburg that columns and orders are not flat surface decoration.

Standing at the two ends of the colonnade are statues of Napoleonic-era military commanders, Kutuzov (on the left as you face the cathedral) and Barclay de Tolly (on the right). They are by sculptor Boris Orlovsky and were put into place in 1837. Kutuzov himself is buried inside the cathedral, which also held the military trophies of the czarist era. During the World War II siege of Leningrad, the Russians were scrupulously careful to sandbag and camouflage great architectural monuments. They even went so far as to assign individual fighter pilots to particular buildings to protect them from bombing raids. Even so, throughout the war Kutuzov and Barclay de Tolly were left uncovered as an inspiration to the city.

The square is also famous as the site of numerous antigovernment demonstrations in the czarist period. "It was always known in advance when the students would riot in front of Kazan Cathedral," the poet Osip Mandelstam described. "Every family had its student informer. The result was that these riots were attended—at a re-

spectful distance, to be sure—by a great mass of people."
Children, nurses, retired civil servants, mamas, and aunts
"unable to keep the insurrectionaries at home" all figured
among the gawkers who waited until the Cossacks swept
down. This game with the authorities turned tragic on
Bloody Sunday in January 1905, when hundreds of dem-
onstrators lost their lives.

The Kazan Cathedral is portentous. It resembles later
buildings in the nineteenth century, like St. Isaac's Cathedral (Walk 7), more than its own contemporaries.
Heavy granite left to weather is far from the delicate yellow and white dress of classical and Empire taste. There
is a spirit almost industrial in the cathedral's might.

Perhaps by virtue of stone it at first glance has something in common with the granite-clad art nouveau
building (1902–04) directly across the street, which is
unabashedly also about the materials of which it is made.
Atlas carries a globe of glass and metal as a crown to the
building, while the writing on the left reads "*Dom Knigi,*"
or House of the Book. It is fitting that Petersburg's avant-
garde architects of the turn of the century (in this instance, Syuzor) felt free to pillage the classical past. The
bronze sculptures mounted on the facade are weirdly
reminiscent of baroque palace incrustations of the eighteenth century. The building still holds Leningrad's largest bookstore, while the upper floors are editorial offices.

The canal that flanks the cathedral is a union of
swamp streams, widened, deepened, and lined with
granite under the reign of Catherine the Great, for whom
it was long named. In 1923 it took the name of Alexander
Griboyedov, a great nineteenth-century playwright and
satirist, who came to a bloody end on diplomatic assign-
ment. Sent to Teheran in 1828 to enforce provisions of
a peace treaty negotiated with Persia, he was killed when
the Russian embassy was sacked by a mob incensed by
the demand that captured Christian women be released
from harems. Griboyedov lived on the embankment. If
you have extra time, trace the crooked canal behind the

Hanging lamps on the Griboyedov Canal

cathedral for several hundred yards. Decorative foot-bridges span the narrow waterway, overhung by trees and mirroring facade and sky. It is one of the loveliest passages in the city.

Notice how the cathedral colonnade lines up perfectly with the canal embankment going in the other direction toward the toylike **Church of the Resurrection of Christ**. In fact, you might try photographing this church from inside the colonnade, where a passageway of pillars frames the toplike cupolas and tiled facade.

Now cross Nevsky Prospect again. We are going to follow the Griboyedov Canal to the Church of the Resurrection, keeping at first to the left embankment. The beige building at #13 with fancy grilles over the windows and an Atlas above the doorway is an earlier work (1888–90) by Syuzor. It served as a bank.

Use the footbridge just ahead to pass to the other side of the canal, and as you cross notice the vista opening down Rakov (formerly Italian) Street. Way down at the end is the portico of the **Catherine Institute** on the Fontanka River, a view which should be familiar from Walk 5. The trees visible in mid-course are those of the **Square of the Arts**, and even buildings on the Griboye-dov Embankment extend all the way to this grand square. At #4 is the back side of the **Maly Theater of Opera and Ballet** while #2 is a wing of the Mikhailovsky Palace, which houses the **Russian Museum**.

This stretch of the canal is dominated by the Church of the Resurrection of Christ (1883–1907). It was built on the spot that Alexander II was mortally wounded by a terrorist bomb on March 1, 1881, hence its better-known popular name, **Church of the Savior on the Blood**. With Bolshevik tact the bridge just behind the church was named for Ignacy Hryniewicky, Alexander's murderer. On the day he was killed the emperor had agreed to a new elective assembly, one of the liberals' long-held demands, but his son Alexander III undid all this. Until 1905 Russia would remain in a period of re-action.

The Church of the Savior on the Blood

174

Along with the *Bronze Horseman* and the Admiralty, this church could stand as a symbol of St. Petersburg. Although built in medieval style, it is a product of the late nineteenth century, when Russians woke to the romance of their history. This church is a romp through the gaudy past, yet it misses the grim potency that made medieval color so bright. Though it marks the spot of a murder, there is no tragedy in the building. It is an ethnographic and art historical game pursued by a group of artists who had patronage and curiosity. It is as far from medieval architecture as Mussorgsky's *Boris Godunov* is from Kremlin power politics of the early seventeenth century.

The architect, P. Parland, was affiliated with the Abramtsevo school (named for the estate of a rich patron), which mined the Russian past. Folk woodcarving techniques were studied along with monuments of medieval architecture. The resulting decorative abandon would lead directly into art nouveau. Victor Vasnetsov, a painter whose name is closely associated with Abramtsevo's innovations, produced the tiles and mosaics for the facade.

Nothing better illustrates the distance between Petersburg and Moscow than to compare this church with its inspiration, Moscow's St. Basil's Cathedral. Moscow's church is full-blooded, a great work of art that encompasses divine menace and decoration, while Petersburg's church is all light charm. It was impossible for a city founded in 1703, a child of the Enlightenment, to grasp Moscow's cruel mystical essence. Yet the northern capital has its own propriety and philosophy. It put stock in architecture as a setting. People (of the proper class) were to live in an elegant environment. Art would appear in mannered social interaction, acting on stage, and the private exercise of writing or composing. Petersburg came of age when this was the most architecture could do. In the eighteenth and nineteenth centuries other art forms were dominant as spiritual forces.

Bear to the right as you walk around the church. On

Parland's grille at the edge of Mikhailovsky Garden

your right is an extravagant wrought-iron fence with floral patterns marking off the grounds of the Mikhailovsky
Palace. Parland was also responsible for this art nouveau
grille (1903–07), one of the finest in the city, completed
in the same years as the church.

By the end of the nineteenth century architecture was
growing more intrusive. It began to leave behind the pas-
sivity that made it an ideal backdrop. True, most aristo-
crats preferred old styles and the up and coming
merchants clung carefully to precedent, but the *au courant*
built in the opulent "millionaire's style," as art nouveau
was often called. Moscow is particularly rich in isolated
fin de siècle mansions, which abandon balance for asymmetry, and Greek orders for the vine. That was in Moscow. Here in Petersburg, art nouveau for the most part
succumbed to the overpowering order of the city. Even
this church (built in the "Russian style" that predated
art nouveau) and the grille simply become *objets d'art*,
losing their subversive force in the midst of Petersburg
grace.

Like the innocuous syllables of a magic spell, the city's bland repetition of columns and orders so bewitches that nothing looks ordinary. Yet this dream is at a price. The spell eviscerates whole buildings and leaves floating details: a rose-gray sky, a gilded spire, and a twisting grille. A great building could be built, but had to join the ensemble of architectural voices, as if Shaliapin had entered a chorus. This is one of the reasons Petersburg is so hard to explain to people who haven't been there. Unlike other cities, it is one work. The classical repetition allows ornate moments to stand forth starkly.

Now it is time for the gardens and parks of which we spoke at the beginning. Walk through the gate on the right and enter the **Mikhailovsky Garden**, following the curving main path. After several hundred feet you will reach a bronze bust mounted on a pink granite pedestal, raised in 1959 to commemorate an architect named Shubin. Behind you is the garden facade of the regal Mikhailovsky Palace, built by Carlo Rossi in 1819–25. This is the palace that fronts the Square of the Arts where Walk 5 concludes. Think of the contrast between this garden and the square and street leading to Nevsky Prospect on the other side. It is as if we were in another world, which was the intention of the architect.

Rossi redesigned the garden in "landscape" or "English" style when he completed the palace. Originally it was an extension of the more formal "French" style Summer Garden, laid out in a geometric pattern, which we will see farther on. But here Rossi wanted a sense of natural irregularity, a private park in which his patron, the Grand Duke Mikhail (the younger brother of Emperors Alexander I and Nicholas I), could relax outside the strictures of order. Of course, the freedom is illusory and all secretly subject to the Petersburg grid.

Follow the path you are on straight across the garden until you reach a fork with two other routes leading off to the left. Take the right of the two (both enter the main path almost at perpendicular) and walk straight down to the yellow and white **Empire Pavilion** (1825) at the end. The architect, Rossi, has made use of a particularly reflective site on the Moika River with granite stairs and a landing for boats below. Notice that the pavilion lines up on an axis with the Mikhailovsky Palace, and then, crossing the river, with the main pathway of the Field of Mars, and farther, with the Kirovsky Bridge across the Neva River. This diminutive little pavilion in a grove acts as a junction between massive ensembles that would normally exist in separation. To the right, across the road and Swan (Lebyazhi) Canal, are the trees of the Summer Garden, a favorite early morning haunt of Pushkin's.

On the **Field of Mars** straight ahead through the screen of trees, Petersburg's secret geometry is sketched out plainly. Four quadrangles, each bisected and then cut by diagonals, surround a central memorial plaza. The gravel pathways speak the geometry we have been noticing throughout the city.

The field is now a monument to "martyrs" of the Revolution and Civil War; newlyweds often stop by here after the marriage ceremony to lay flowers on the tombstones. But the field's martial associations long predate the twentieth century. In 1801 a monument (visible on a traffic island in front of the Kirovsky Bridge) was raised to Russia's great Field Marshal Suvorov in the guise of Mars, whence the current name of the patterned green, or by winter, blanketed white. Like Kutuzov and Barclay de Tolly on Kazansky Square, Suvorov was also left uncovered through the siege of Leningrad. At the very beginning of the eighteenth century, the site was used as a drill ground for soldiers, a practice which was revived a century later for full dress parades after the field had become one of the city's most elegant promenades.

In the 1710s, Peter the Great closed off the field from the surrounding city by digging the **Swan (Lebyazhi) Canal** on the right and the Beautiful (Krasny) Canal, since filled in, on the left to link up the Neva and Moika rivers. No bridges were built, so visitors to the gardens Peter laid out had to come by boat, a reinforcement of the legal requirement that all citizens but the very poorest own private means of water transport. The dock at the base of the pavilion makes more sense when you realize the importance of waterways to the imperial capital.

Now follow the pathway to the right (as you face the river). It runs parallel to the Moika for a stretch and then curves sharply to the right. Exit the garden at the gate that appears on the left. The street you are on is the Large Garden Street (Sadovaya Ulitsa). Directly across from us is the spired **Mikhailovsky Castle** (1797–1800), also known as the Engineering Castle, designed by Vasily Bazhenov and Vincent Brenna. Fairly isolated among the trees, this fortress-palace has a spooky reputation despite the reddish warmth of the facade. Legend has it that the color was chosen by Emperor Paul on the basis of a lady's glove he noticed at a ball: he asked her to give it to him and then sent it to his paint makers to match.

This castle was Paul's obsession for almost the entire duration of his reign. He commissioned it because he did not feel secure in the Winter Palace, and it was the top construction project of the period. Work went on twenty-four hours a day, summer as well as winter, and at night it flared with torches and hissing lanterns. From three to six thousand laborers, pushed mercilessly to speed the work, were on the site at any given moment. Other palaces that had been raised by Catherine the Great were looted of stone and building materials to placate imperial impatience, and in just over three and a half years the Mikhailovsky Castle was finished, the most expensive Russian palace of the eighteenth century.

It was just the place for a frightened monarch. The walls were enormously thick, it was surrounded by a moat (now filled in) with drawbridges drawn up at night, and protective cannon were hidden behind the decorative exterior. As a fortress it was successful, but the rapid building proved to have been shoddy. The interior was drafty, damp, and almost impossible to heat. The walls became so cold in the winter that they were faced over in wood, and even that did little good.

While his family froze, perhaps Paul took comfort in the vision that had inspired the castle in the first place. One night the Archangel Michael is said to have appeared to a soldier standing guard at the Summer Garden across from the site now occupied by the castle, and demanded that a church be built there in his name. When the vision was reported to the superstitious emperor, he answered, "The desire of the Archangel Michael is already known to me, and his will shall be done." Perhaps it was hubris for Paul to build a castle where there should have been a church; in any event, there was a chapel dedicated to the Archangel Michael inside the new residence.

When Ivan III built the Moscow Kremlin in the 1480s and 1490s, he was justly frightened of foreign invaders; Paul built this castle three hundred years later to resist, not invasion, but an uprising by the destitute or a palace coup by his own courtiers. The French Revolution had shocked him. So had the murder of his father, Peter III, with the complicity of Catherine. Paul was a man who lived in fear and yet so terrorized his associates that they were driven to desperation. "The nobleman is he to whom I am speaking, and his nobility lasts only as long as I am speaking to him," is a famous pronouncement of his.

His greatest mistake was to humiliate the military. Like Peter III he was infatuated with Prussian military discipline and uniforms. As soon as he took the throne he forced Russian soldiers to dress like Prussians, provoking Field Marshal Suvorov to retort: "Russians always beat the Prussians, so what are these changes for?" To prepare for review, soldiers had to comb out their hair the night before, dress it with flour and salt, plait it, and then sleep sitting up so as not to mess the hairdo. In the enlisted barracks rats would sometimes try to eat the floured hair. On top went huge tricornered hats that the wind often sent flying. The slightest error in dress or drill could result in immediate exile to Siberia for commanders, hence officers said goodbye to their families and packed extra food and linen every time they turned out.

Everyone felt Paul's regimental imagination. He slept early, so the lights in all windows had to be out by 8:00 P.M.; by 9:00 all street traffic was forbidden except for priests and midwives. He even dictated the number of courses his subjects' dinners could consist of, based on rank (a major, for example, was permitted a three-course dinner).

Just forty-one days after Paul moved into his impregnable castle, all the defenses were breached by drunken conspirators, very senior officials who bluffed their way past guards in the middle of the night, in one case by convincing a sentry that he had fallen asleep and that it was 6:00 A.M. and time to deliver the emperor his morning report. One of the two Hussars guarding Paul's door fled and the other died fighting at his post. Inside the bedroom the emperor was found hiding behind a tapestry, his nightmare come true: he was strangled by officers he had cashiered. In another room his son Alexander waited anxiously for news, having endorsed the coup on the condition his father's life be spared. When he discovered the truth the twenty-three-year-old heir almost refused the throne, but was pressured into taking over, at which the city exploded in celebration.

Alexander I's first gesture was to abandon the castle, and it lay empty and dank for twenty years, accumulating mystery. In the 1820s it was finally turned over to the Department of Military Engineers as a school and barracks, whence its second name as the Engineering Castle. Later in the nineteenth century, from 1838 to 1841, the drafty keep had a resident engineering student who would become even more famous than Paul—Fyodor Dostoyevsky.

Walk now to the left (as we face the castle) down Garden Street (Sadovaya Ulitsa) until you cross the **Garden Bridge** (Sadoviy Most) over the Moika River. As you cross, over your shoulder you'll have a good view of Rossi's pavilion on the Moika. Above the trees are the swirling spires and gilded crosses of the Church of Savior on the Blood where Alexander II was murdered, and on the right side of the river is an open view of the Field of Mars. On the bridge, take special note of the lanterns that are decorated with the martial wreaths and arrows typical of Empire style.

Once you cross the bridge, keep to your right until you reach the entrance to the **Summer Garden**. Notice the Medusae heads "reflected" in the medallions mounted on the fence (circa 1820) designed by L. I. Charlemagne II. It is here at the gates that the soldier had the vision of the Archangel Michael that inspired the Mikhailovsky Castle, looming grandly across the water. Before entering the Summer Garden, continue on just ahead to the next waterway, the Fontanka, intersecting the Moika River. The bridge over the Fontanka (named for the fountains which once filled the Summer Garden) offers lovely views in both directions: reaching the Neva River on the left, and heading toward the city center on the right.

St. Petersburg is a city of the north. Until 1918 it was the northernmost capital of any country in the world, and it remains by far the largest metropolitan center at this latitude. Nature here has a rugged and tempestuous force, from icy winter winds off the Neva to the breakup of frozen rivers in the spring. It is hard to imagine a region more different from the Mediterranean climate of Italy with its clambering grapes and idle ruins. Yet Italy, along with Versailles, inspired the Summer Garden.

This garden was one of Peter the Great's obsessions, and an early geometric plan is sometimes credited to him. In the middle of military campaigns he would scrawl orders for new trees: from Moscow, Siberia, Persia, or tropical India. Bananas and pineapples were tended in an orangerie that once stood along the Fontanka. By Russian tradition, gardens grew food for the table, and the *ogorod* (vegetable garden) was something all had in common, from czar to serf. Yet Peter also commissioned magnificent fountains, and imported seventeenth-century Italian outdoor statuary to decorate the modern alleys. The fountains have long been removed but the statues remain. Peter's proudest acquisition, a second-century Roman Venus for which he posted a special guard, now resides in the Hermitage.

"Classicism became a genuine national style in our

The Goddess Ceres in the Summer Garden

country," insists a Russian art historian. The claim has merit, and not simply because Petersburg's buildings *look* classical. It is in little things that a sensibility reveals itself. The big things can be faked through strenuous efforts. A czar determined to join an alien civilization could have ordered up convincing copies. But such strident efforts would have rung strange, like a bell cast with too many metals. Petersburg rings clear with a classicism purified. The Summer Garden's baroque statues are imported from Italy, but they have adapted to local ground, local trees, and even the diffused light of the northern sun.

It is time to enter the gate. Directly in front of us is the **Karpiev Pond**, very close to its original form as a basin draining surrounding swampland. From 1714 to 1716 it was deepened and lined, along with the digging of canals. At the same time this drainage system was laid, the low-lying land was heavily built up for the reception of trees and plants. Like so much else in the city, the Summer Garden to its very soil is an invention.

Follow the **Main Alley (Glavnaya Alleiya)** straight into the park from the right side of the pond. The trees have reached a mature height, and while the alleys evoke some order of the past, in Peter's time the garden was far more formal, tiered with flowers, fragrant bushes, wooden pavilions, over fifty fountains, trees (oak, maple, linden, elm, ash, fir, chestnut, apple, pear), and bushes groomed in the style of Versailles or spilling with berries. Already by the middle of the eighteenth century the garden was well along in its transformation to current appearance. By the time Pushkin composed poetry here in his bathrobe in the early morning, it looked much as it does now.

Continue down the Main Alley until you reach the statuary—here the spirits of the pagan past linger among the trees. Next to the Swan Canal, Cupid rouses Psyche from languorous sleep on a fabulous bed; on the Main Alley, Ceres gathers the harvest with the grace of a woman at a ball. This is a paganism of the elegant and idle. It is ironic that the stone gods were bought from the south.

The Summer Palace

Just over a century before Peter took the throne, the Russian Church was still extirpating paganism in the remote northern forests, including the region that would later become Petersburg. Clerics cut down sacred groves, burnt temples to the ground, and smashed sacred stones where human sacrifice took place, the chroniclers darkly charged. One holy site was about 10 kilometers from here. The Italian garden statues were a paganism of the intellect rather than the heart, but nevertheless undoubtedly provoked the church. Peter was seeking a new ideology to image his ambition, and classical mythology was to symbolize the grandeur of his reign.

We see this political classicism, as opposed to the garden variety, on the facade of the **Summer Palace** (1710–14), built by Domenico Trezzini as one of the earliest stone buildings in Petersburg. To reach the palace, walk to the far right corner of the garden, where the Neva and the Fontanka rivers meet, one of the most idyllic spots in the city. From its founding in 1703, Petersburg's inhospitality was not merely in climate and terrain. The marshy site was militarily exposed and Russia was engaged with Sweden in the long and bloody Northern War (1700–10). The Summer Palace was be-

gun only after Russia decisively won the Battle of Pol-
tava in 1709 and the siege of Vyborg in 1710. With
them came unchallenged access to the Baltic Sea and the
rest of Europe. The bas-relief sculptures on the facade
of the pale yellow, two-story Summer Palace celebrate
the successful war in allegorical form.

The images are rather obscure. For example, a relief
panel on the east wall (facing the Fontanka) showing a
putto battling with a "sea elephant" is a reference to a
naval battle in which the Swedish flagship was named
The Elephant. In the myth of Atalanta on the south wall
(facing into the garden), a suitor is required to outrun the
beautiful maiden to wed her; he throws golden apples at
her feet and thus wins the race by distracting her. The
parallel was with the early stage of the Northern War.
Instead of following up a decisive victory over Russia at
Narva, Sweden chose to pursue the "golden apple" of a
campaign in Poland, which gave Peter the Great time to
rebuild his army and strike back. Water is a favorite
theme, since Peter was obsessed with naval power and
trade routes to the West. Compared to buildings of only
ten years before in Moscow, it is astonishing how Westernized the Summer Palace is in symbolism.

Tickets to go inside (open from noon to 8:00 P.M.
May through November, and closed Tuesdays) are available at the wooden Chainy Domik (Tea House) that lies
just to the south of the palace and farther in from the
Fontanka. The Tea House was built in 1827 by L. I. Charlemagne II, also the designer of the southern grille to the
garden; unfortunately, it no longer purveys tea. The large
bronze sculpture of a man reading a book in front of the
Tea House is a portrait of Ivan Krylov, a great writer of
fables. Characters from his stories populate the base of
the sculpture, designed in 1855 by P. K. Klodt.

From its completion, Peter lived in the palace every
year from May until October, until his death in 1725.
The palace (in Petrine Baroque style) does not compare
in scale or cost with Rastrelli's extravagances of forty years

later, like the Winter Palace or Peterhof. But it is a clear declaration of intent. Modeled architecturally on the residences of Dutch burghers, the interior assimilates Western art and science. Within lies a strange German clock contraption that also measured wind speed, a machine designed to copy engraving plates, a kitchen with Dutch tiles and the first plumbing in Petersburg, and human organs preserved in glass bottles filled with alcohol. The latter specimens rest on shelves in the Green Cabinet on the second floor, the only room of the palace to retain all of its original decoration. The other rooms have been restored based on plans, documents, and the accounts of contemporaries.

Make sure to look out the windows from the pink ballroom on the second floor. The view sweeps over the black-banded and golden-sphered **northern gates** to the Neva. Like the grille on the Griboyedov Canal, this also marks the site of a terrorist attack on Alexander II. In 1866, fifteen years before he was to lose his life to a bomb, he was shot at but not injured while leaving the park. A plaque to the would-be assassin, Dmitri Karakozov, was hung on the gate in 1931 at the same time a chapel on the spot was torn down.

It is at these gates, designed by Yuri Felten in 1773–84, that we are going to conclude this walk. We have spoken of the classical backdrop that the city offers, allowing decorative details to flare into life. Here it is the wide sky above the Neva that is the backdrop, and the grille's gold, black, and granite trace magnificently. Somehow the opalescent yonder finds eighteenth-century refinement congenial. How this can be is a mystery. One would think that the wind and cold of the north would find Italian indolence and French delicacy an affront, but the extremes have married. St. Petersburg is unique both for its architectural purity and for the omnipresent voice of nature. Perhaps in proportion and Greek orders there lies a truth nature recognizes.

Walk · 7

Along the Left Bank of the Neva

Ship's bow on a Rostral Column

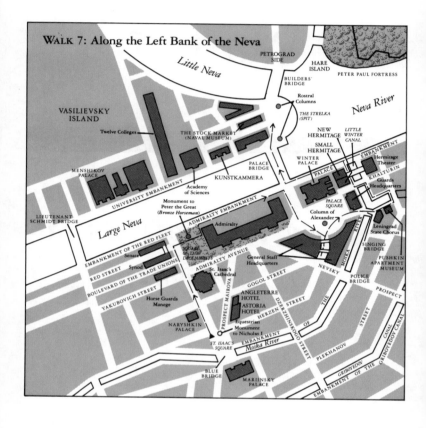

WALK 7: Along the Left Bank of the Neva

PETROGRAD SIDE

HARE ISLAND

PETER PAUL FORTRESS

Little Neva

BUILDERS' BRIDGE

Rostral Columns

THE STRELKA (SPIT)

Neva River

VASILIEVSKY ISLAND

Twelve Colleges

THE STOCK MARKET (NAVAL MUSEUM)

NEW HERMITAGE

LITTLE WINTER CANAL

PALACE BRIDGE

WINTER PALACE

SMALL HERMITAGE

Hermitage Theater

EMBANKMENT

MENSHIKOV PALACE

KUNSTKAMMERA

Academy of Sciences

PALACE

KHALTURIN

Guards Headquarters

UNIVERSITY EMBANKMENT

Monument to Peter the Great (Bronze Horseman)

ADMIRALTY EMBANKMENT

PALACE SQUARE

Column of Alexander

LIEUTENANT SCHMIDT BRIDGE

Large Neva

Admiralty

Leningrad State Chorus

MOIKA RIVER

SINGING BRIDGE

EMBANKMENT OF THE RED FLEET

SQUARE OF 14TH DECEMBER 1825

NEVSKY

PUSHKIN APARTMENT MUSEUM

Senate

ADMIRALTY AVENUE

General Staff Headquarters

POLICE BRIDGE

PROSPECT

RED STREET

Synod

BOULEVARD OF THE TRADE UNIONS

St. Isaac's Cathedral

GOGOL STREET

DZERZHINSKOGO STREET

THE

YAKUBOVICH STREET

Horse Guards Manege

ANGLETERRE HOTEL

ASTORIA HOTEL

HERZEN STREET

STREET

GRIBOYEDOV CANAL

NARYSHKIN PALACE

Equestrian Monument to Nicholas I

EMBANKMENT

Moika River

PLEKHANOV

PROSPECT MAIROVA

ST. ISAAC'S SQUARE

BLUE BRIDGE

MARIINSKY PALACE

EMBANKMENT OF THE GRIBOYEDOV CANAL

Starting Point: St. Isaac's Square
Walk Length: 3 hours

There is no metro stop near St. Isaac's Square. If you use public transportation, take the metro to the Griboyedov Canal entrance of the Gostinniy Dvor stop (where Walk 6 began). From there you can take a trolleybus (#5 or 14) or a bus (#3, 22, or 27) down Nevsky Prospect in the direction of the Admiralty. Both will turn off Nevsky to the left before reaching St. Isaac's Square.

When Peter the Great established a fortress on the Neva River in 1703, he was acting out of military necessity in the Northern War with Sweden. Within months his thoughts coursed more grandly, to the idea of making this outpost of a bloody conflict his capital. It was an idea that appealed to few of his subjects. The dim, marshy land, so far north that the sun hung eerily on the horizon through the midsummer night, was old Russian demesne. But it had been lost to Sweden ninety years earlier and Peter's successful war to get it back hardly lessened its isolation and fearfulness.

The rise of St. Petersburg astonished Russians. In 1712, when its stone buildings could still be counted on fingers, Peter made it his capital. Tens of thousands of his subjects, from nobles down to serfs, were forced to locate here, often to die from pneumonia or tuberculosis. The city rose out of the mist with the rapidity of a dream.

Perhaps more surprising than Petersburg's magical appearance is that a city had not always existed here. The Neva had been the gateway to commerce in the Slavic interior at least since the eighth century, and probably much longer. In the ninth century the Varangians (Vikings) traversed this point on the approach to Kiev, where they later established the Rurikid dynasty (whose descendants would rule Muscovy until 1598). Even after the Mongols devastated most of Russia in the thirteenth century, the principality of Novgorod continued lucrative exchange down the Neva and to the Baltic Sea with the cities of the Hanseatic League. Peter understood the advantages of this opening to the sea, and chose to build here a monument to his reign rather than a grimy port. It is as if the beauty of centuries of building that should have been was compressed into the decades that were. Petersburg flowered on stone piles in a swamp because of the natural virtue of the Neva. The will of emperors concentrated enormous wealth here, but megalomania alone does not explain the city's success.

The interior of St. Petersburg is grand, but the monuments on the Neva embankment are superlative, bathed by the soft light of flowing water and open sky. Here lie the residences of the grand dukes and czars. The river is wide so that from either side the opposite bank traces a rhythmic silhouette of domes, spires, and columns. Gilt catches the light of hour and palaces rest beneath, with regiments of fine pilasters standing guard. Living off the labor of serfs who constituted half the population, the tiny Russian aristocracy built a culture that could have passed for Elysium.

The perfect taste of the city is never stained by visible blood, but the threat of violence for both ruler and ruled often hung near. Throughout his reign Peter the Great was faced with opposition, and suffered the ultimate indignity of having his son Alexei turn against him. Alexei was put to death, by the czar himself some whispered. After Peter's death in 1725, for the rest of the eighteenth century it was the Guards regiments that determined who held power. Empresses Catherine I, Anna, Elizabeth, and Catherine II all owed their crowns to the support of Russia's Praetorians.

We mention violence because it was so central to the reign (1825–56) of Nicholas I, who is celebrated in the square where we begin our walk. We are not far from the Neva, and indeed St. Isaac's Cathedral plays a glittering role on the skyline as seen from the embankment. But for now we should focus our attention on the **equestrian statue** in the middle of the square. It is a monument to Nicholas I built in 1856–59 by Auguste Montferrand (architect of St. Isaac's) immediately after the emperor's death. It is hard to imagine a monument more in keeping with Nicholas's character: black, monumental, and fear-inspiring. The horse was cast by P. K. Klodt, the same sculptor who produced the rearing horses for the Anichkov Bridge (Walk 5). The four female figures beneath the mounted Nicholas are Faith, Wisdom, Justice, and Strength, while the bas-relief plaques set in red granite render the major events of his reign.

St. Isaac's Cathedral (1818–58), toward which Nicholas seems to canter, is also a monument to his reign. The construction spanned his rule, and the cathedral is the architectural equivalent of "Autocracy, Orthodox, and Nationality," the ideology that lay at the basis of his policy. "Autocracy" refers to the necessity of the absolute monarchy, "Orthodoxy" to the faith which Russia received from Byzantium and now protected, and "Nationality" to the special destiny of the Russian people. Catholic Poles, Lutheran Finns, Jews, and Moslem subjects or neighbors were the great losers in this vision.

With five cupolas, St. Isaac's Cathedral observes the rule that patriarch Nikon laid down in 1655—that a church had to have one, three, or five cupolas. Yet this is an orthodoxy adapted to the nineteenth century: it wears classical dress. Fifteenth-century churches in the Moscow Kremlin also absorb foreign styles and retain

intact an Orthodox religious heart, the multitiered iconostasis.

Even stranger, St. Isaac's Cathedral is a product of the industrial revolution, which allowed the lifting of columns weighing over 100 tons; a metal carcass for the massive central cupola (a technique borrowed by the builders of the U.S. Capitol); and the first use of galvanization to preserve metals outdoors. St. Isaac's swells out of the scale intended for classical buildings, but it does embody the stolid spirit of Nicholas's Russia. No expense was spared. The interior is sheathed with gilded bronze and stone from across the empire: lapus lazuli, malachite, and colored granites and marbles. When completed it became the main cathedral in the city.

It is no wonder that the cathedral took forty years to build. Auguste Montferrand, the architect, was confronted with multiple layers of review at every stage of the construction, in which both church and state participated. Emperor Nicholas himself was deeply involved with the project and often interfered with technical and aesthetic questions about which he knew little, thus further slowing the pace. Rumors circulated that the Romanov family would fall when St. Isaac's was completed, and that the czar was reluctant to see the work come to an end. It finally did in 1858, two years after Nicholas I had died.

It is now a museum open from 11:00 A.M. until 5:00 P.M. every day except Wednesday. If you visit make sure to get tickets also to the balcony (pronounced *bal-KON*), from which there is a spectacular view of the city.

The first wooden St. Isaac's Cathedral was built nearby in 1710, and was named for the saint marking Peter the Great's birthday. It stood on the spot now taken by the *Bronze Horseman*, a famous monument to Peter which we will see shortly. In 1717–27 a stone church was built on this site, but it soon turned out that the river was too close for the good of the foundation. Finally, in

St. Isaac's Cathedral

1762, under the patronage of Catherine the Great, work was begun on a refined baroque cathedral by Antonio Rinaldi that occupied the current site. It was virtually completed when Catherine died and Paul came to power. Partly out of spite for his mother, he used the marble sheathing at the top of the cathedral to dress his obsession, the Mikhailovsky Castle, which we saw in Walk 6.

The half-dressed St. Isaac's Cathedral became the butt of bitter jokes, and late one night a young naval officer was caught attaching a rhyme to the facade:

> This monument to two reigns,
> Both of them so proper:
> The foundation of one has marble veins
> And brick at the top of the other.

Paul had the officer's tongue and ears sliced off, before he was exiled to Siberia. Yet for over twenty years the embarrassing monument remained, until Montferrand received his commission.

There is another tale of violence associated with this cathedral, only this time it took place during the reign of Nicholas. The Senate Square lies on the Neva side of the church, and it was the site of the Decembrist uprising against Nicholas's accession to the throne in 1825. Often, the revolt is viewed as a romantic effort by Westernized officers, out of touch with the sentiments of common people. Be that as it may, during the insurrection when Nicholas attempted to approach the Senate Square from the St. Isaac's side, he was charged by laborers who threw beams at him. A subsequent police investigation was able to find out nothing.

Directly across the square from the cathedral is the **Mariinsky Palace** (1839–44) by Andrei Shtackenshneider, another example of how classicism's delicate proportions were left behind as the nineteenth century progressed. The palace was originally built for Nicholas I's eldest daughter, Maria, although forty years later it went to the State Council (Russia's legislature). From March through July 1917 the palace served the Provisional Government, which had replaced the monarchy, but after the October Revolution it was turned over to the Leningrad Soviet. It now houses the Executive Committee of the Leningrad Soviet, which is under the control of democrats.

Much of the plaza in front of the palace is actually the (Blue) Siniy Bridge over the Moika, the widest in the city. To your right (as you face the palace) on the right embankment of the Moika is an obelisk that marks by year the heights the city's floods have reached. The marker is a striking lesson in the city's vulnerability to water.

Now turn back to face St. Isaac's Cathedral. One of Leningrad's best pre-Revolutionary hotels, the **Astoria** (1911–12), is located on the right at the corner of Herzen Street and has long been under renovation. During the October Revolution it was stormed by Bolshevik troopers, who fought a brief battle with cadets and officers sheltering inside. The next building down toward the Neva was the less expensive **Angleterre Hotel**, where the poet Sergei Esenin, married to Isadora Duncan, hung himself in 1925. Not long ago the pale red hotel was at the center of a dispute over restoration, with many arguing that it should retain the appearance it had in Esenin's time (when many other avant-garde poets and artists stayed there as well). After a city-wide referendum, the hotel, which had already been fully renovated, was restored to its original appearance.

Incidentally, notice how the view down **Prospect Maiorova** (running past the two hotels) is concluded by the central spire of the Admiralty. This is the same vista we noticed down Nevsky Prospect in Walk 5, since Maiorova is one of the three main avenues converging on the Admiralty. The third avenue to do this, Dzerzhinskogo (formerly Gorokhovaya) lies equidistant between Nevsky and Maiorova.

Now walk to the left side of the square (as you face the cathedral). Opposite the Astoria Hotel, the sober granite building with attached columns at **#11** was built at exactly the same time (1911–12) as the Astoria Hotel and served as the German embassy until the war. It is now Intourist's Leningrad headquarters.

The salmon-colored building next door with medallions and friezes on the facade is the **Naryshkin Palace** (1760s) by Antonio Rinaldi, one of Catherine the Great's favorite architects. Denis Diderot stayed here on a visit to Russia in 1773 at the invitation of the empress. Just as Peter the Great imported classical mythology as his official ideology, Catherine II looked to the West and came up with the stirring rhetoric of the French Enlightenment. With the flowery support of the Great Skeptics—Voltaire, Diderot, and others—Catherine managed to create the world's first chic autocracy. Diderot did become disillusioned by the end of his four-month stay. But Russia has long suffered the misfortune of being the land in which discontented Europeans (and later Americans) have seen their political fantasies played out. At least Nicholas I's ideology of "Autocracy, Orthodoxy, and Nationality" was a more honest explanation of his behavior.

In the realm of culture and architecture, Catherine did sponsor a Petersburg of reason and the golden mean. No doubt Diderot was as impressed by his residence, whose interior is well preserved, as he was by the perfect French and politically correct speech of the empress. The architect Rinaldi was also designer of the baroque St. Isaac's Cathedral going up alongside, which later lost its marbles to the Mikhailovsky Castle.

It is a revealing irony that the very months Diderot was passing the time in Petersburg, Catherine was facing Pugachev's Peasant Rebellion, which nearly reached the dimensions of Stenka Razin's revolt of 130 years earlier, before its leader was put down and quartered on Red Square. Pugachev's success in raising armies of tens of thousands was fed by the brutality of serfdom and autocracy, yet there is no trace of savagery in Petersburg's palaces. Wealth and power permitted the creation of a visual utopia, the most successful propaganda of Catherine's reign.

If you compare the Naryshkin Palace with the new cathedral and other buildings on the square, you get a clear sense of how much the ensemble changed through the nineteenth century. St. Isaac's Square today is dramatic, but it lacks the exquisite symmetries classical architects were able to conceive. Under Nicholas I and his successors, the outward appearance of buildings remained traditional, but scale and technology swelled.

The building two doors further down at #5 houses the **Museum of Musical Instruments**, open noon until 6:00 P.M. every day except Monday and Tuesday. Instruments used by composers such as Glinka, Dorgomizhsky, Borodin, and Rimsky-Korsakov are on display.

Ahead you can see the Neva River, the raison d'être of the city. But we have a few more buildings to which we should pay heed before reaching the embankment. As we leave St. Isaac's Square we retreat back into the early nineteenth century when most of the Senate Square (now known as the Square of the Decembrists) was laid out. It is here that the Russian monarchy learned the true consequences of the Age of Enlightenment that Catherine had so glibly embraced.

On your left across Yakubovich Street is the austere **Horse Guards Manege** (1804–07) by Giacomo Quarenghi. This building played an even more important role in the layout of the city for the first seventy years of its life. Until the Admiralty gardens to the right were planted in 1872–74, the manege completed an open vista all the way from the Palace Square over a mile away. The simplicity of Quarenghi's design makes sense when you consider the length of this perspective line. The stark columns and triangular crown would have played well against the deep, evenly spaced shadows of the portico, when seen from such a distance. The marble sculptures out front, of

The Bronze Horseman

rearing horses being restrained by young men, were copied in 1817 by P. Triscorni from the Quirinale Palace in Rome.

Adjacent to the manege on the river side is the **Trade Unions Boulevard** (Bulvar Profsoyuzov), which originally had the more romantic name of Horse Guards Boulevard. The street and the two granite columns crowned by sculptures of Victory were designed by Rossi in 1845–46, to replace an old canal that was then filled in.

Straight ahead of us lies the **Senate Square** (renamed the Square of the Decembrists in 1925), dominated by Leningrad's most famous monument, Etienne Falconet's equestrian statue of Peter the Great. This is the *Bronze Horseman* that received its name from a poem of Pushkin's. The statue was commissioned by Catherine the Great in 1768–82 as a tribute to the czar she most admired. The plain inscription on the base links her reign to his:

Along the Left Bank of the Neva

For a period in which sculpture was largely sterile and imitative, Falconet created a masterpiece of drama and spare expression. The classically robed and laurel-crowned figure may not be literally Peter, but there could be no better image of the ideal monarch of the eighteenth century. Naturalism in the portraiture and clifflike pedestal fuses with the ideal. The pedestal was designed by Yuri Felten, who would go on to produce the granite embankment of the Neva River. Two of Falconet's students cast Peter's head (Marie Collot) and the snake (Fyodor Gordeev).

The *Bronze Horseman* was even more central to the city when it marked the approach to the single bridge across the Neva, a pontoon that was removed in the winter. The Senate Square was then the first ensemble to meet people crossing over from the other side.

It is here that 3,000 rebellious soldiers from the Guard massed on December 14, 1825, in a challenge to the new Emperor Nicholas, one of the most romantic and tragic chapters in Russian history. Technically, not Nicholas but his brother Konstantin should have taken the throne. But by secret agreement Konstantin had renounced power. This left Nicholas in difficulty when Alexander I unexpectedly died, because Konstantin's renunciation had never been made public. Hence Nicholas pledged allegiance to Konstantin, but his brother steadfastly refused the realm. After two weeks Nicholas finally announced plans for his own coronation, but in the eyes of many he was a usurper.

The officers leading the revolt took advantage of the dynastic crisis to push for reforms they had long desired. They were among the best educated men Russia had ever produced, and many were veterans of the Napoleonic Wars. As members of the gentry class they benefited more than anyone, except for the emperor and his family, from Russia's inequities, yet they sought a true republic. Their manifesto called for the abolition of both monarchy and serfdom, and for the convening of a Constituent Assembly to draft a new constitution. Some of the Decembrists were inspired by the example of George Washington and the American Revolution, while others identified with the original goals of the French Republic. As George Kennan eloquently observed in a famous essay published at the height of the cold war, "There is no liberal tradition finer than the strain which existed in the Russia of the past. Many Russian individuals and groups are deeply imbued with that tradition, and will do all in their power to make it the dominant element in the Russian future." Undoubtedly, he had the Decembrists, among others, in mind when he wrote that passage.

Unlike successful palace coups of the past guided by more selfish motives, this one was badly planned, particularly in the sense that no effort was made to capture Nicholas himself. The czar had no trouble rallying loyal regiments with which he surrounded the hapless revolutionaries. A cavalry charge was unsuccessful, so on the day of his coronation, Nicholas ordered the cannon to fire.

The investigations that followed terrorized almost the entire intelligentsia and set the tone for Nicholas's thirty-year reign. The five leaders of the revolt (Pavel Pestel, Petr Kakhovsky, Kondraty Ryleev, Sergei Muravev-Apostol, and Mikhail Bestuzhev-Riumin) were sentenced to death. In three cases the nooses slipped during the hanging, and the men fell to the scaffold. By tradition, they should have been spared, but Nicholas ordered that they be hung again. Hundreds were exiled to hard labor in Siberia, including the sons of many of Russia's oldest noble families. It was not until after Nicholas's death in 1856 that the few survivors were pardoned and allowed to return west.

The complex by Carlo Rossi on the left side of the square (as you face the river) went up in 1829–34 in the gloomy years of repression that followed the Decembrists' revolt. Yet there is not a trace of tragedy in the column-encrusted facade. Sometimes architecture expresses inhumanity in what it does not express. Russia's medieval cathedrals are decorative, frightening, and sublime. Rossi does not have such range; his agenda is order, not the unpredictable flare of spontaneous creation. To the left of the giant archway was housed the Church Synod, and to the right the Senate, both strengthening imperium. The whole complex is now a branch of the Central Historical Archives.

Be sure to look back toward St. Isaac's Cathedral from the square. Especially when the flowerbeds are in bloom it is very lovely, with distance lightening its monolithic weight.

In the summer the Senate Square loses some of its coherence because of the screen of trees that blocks a view of the **Admiralty facade**, directly across from the Senate and Synod. Walk over to the Admiralty side of the square and take a close look at the building, which was built by Adrian Zakharov in 1806–23. It is just as much a symbol of Petersburg as is the *Bronze Horseman*. As soon as Peter established the **Peter Paul Fortress** (visible upriver to the right), he laid out wharfs and a shipbuilding yard on this side of the Neva. The complex was protected by ramparts and wooden bastions, whose positions are now marked by Zakharov's Empire-style creation.

From the Senate Square we look at only one minor facade (163 meters or about 180 yards long) of the building. Another facade duplicating this one faces the Winter Palace, which we will see shortly. The main facade runs for 407 meters (about 445 yards) along Admiralty Street to the right. Its center is marked by the famous spire on which the left bank's three main avenues converge. This spire is the only remnant of an earlier Admiralty (1732–38) by Ivan Korobov, which Zakharov's work replaced.

Like the Summer Palace of 100 years earlier (Walk 6)

the Admiralty has allegorical sculptures. Above the archway in the middle of the main facade, Neptune gives
Peter a trident to symbolize his dominion over the seas.
The symbolism works in a more literal sense, too. As
many have pointed out, the administrative offices of the
Admiralty surrounded the shipyard; the din of building,
and of ships loading and unloading, must have been
present to officials all day long. The elegant facade
screened the hard labor of the wharfs. It also marked the
transition from regal streets to the lifeline of the city, the
Neva itself.

The Admiralty not only screens the Neva, it interprets
it. At the base of the main spire are two famous sculptural
groups by Fyodosy Shchredin—*Sea Nymphs Supporting the
World* (1812–13). The city was founded on the Neva to
provide access to the sea, and the classical age required
mythological equivalents. Sea nymphs support the world
and for Russia the Admiralty rules the sea. If you have
extra time, we suggest pacing the main facade of the Admiralty from the Winter Palace side, which we reach
shortly.

Now walk down to the **Admiralty pavilion** overlooking the embankment. The archway facing the Neva
marks the route of a canal that encircled the interior shipyard before leaving via an identical pavilion on the other
side. Ships were first floated inside the Admiralty walls
before they were guided down to the river. In the mid-
nineteenth century the wharfs and shipyard were destroyed and the canal filled in. The land inside was
auctioned off in the 1860s and 1870s to private developers
who built the grandiose townhouse palaces that now line
the road along the river, here known as the **Admiralty
Embankment** (Admiralteiskaya Naberezhnaya).

Cross over to the river's edge. The Neva has been
more of a threat to the city than one would imagine on
placid days. As recently as 1924 and 1975, huge terri-
tories have lain underwater. Yet in the eighteenth century
the danger lay not simply in floods that swept away

wooden homes, livestock, and people, and destroyed the lower floors of stone dwellings; water seeped and oozed everywhere, and mist breached even homes designed for a cold climate. So the river's granite walls (1762–88) are not simply an aesthetic, but equally a sanitary achievement. Their designer, Yuri Felten, was also responsible for the northern grille to the Summer Garden and the pedestal for the *Bronze Horseman*.

The Neva itself is nature untamed and goes through a yearly drama of freezing, cracking into grinding ice floes, and melting into a crinkled mirror of molten sky. Its endless wardrobe of gowns and jewelry far outshines that of the most extravagant empress. By right, the palaces at the water's edge should have been bested, but they too benefit in the reflected light and seem to change their dress as often as the river and sky.

From the Admiralty Embankment we have a superb view of some of the oldest buildings in the city. This is because **Vasilievsky Island** directly across from us was originally intended to serve as the center of St. Petersburg. It is here that Aleksandr Menshikov (who began as a stable boy, and by virtue of friendship to Peter the Great became the second most powerful man in Russia) built the first stone palace in the city in 1710. The **Menshikov Palace** (three stories, painted yellow with white details) is directly across the river from the Senate. It is a classic example of the spare Petrine Baroque style of Petersburg's first decades, and is now a museum open every day except Monday from 10:30 A.M. to 4:30 P.M. (last entry at 3:00).

Three buildings farther in our direction is the red facade with white details of the **Twelve Colleges**, also in Petrine Baroque style, built in 1722–41 by Dominico Trezzini (designer of the Summer Palace), one of the first foreign architects to come to work for Peter. What we can see is only a tiny portion of the structure, one of the twelve connected "colleges" that stretch lengthwise back from the river. The corridor linking them inside provides

Gulls in front of the Twelve Colleges

a spectacular enfilade view of half a kilometer. Although the Twelve Colleges are now part of Leningrad University, they originally housed the twelve departments (each called a *kollegia*) of the Russian government as Peter organized it in 1718.

After the interval of trees, the next building on the right is the **Academy of Sciences**, built in 1783–88 by Giacomo Quarenghi. On Walk 5 we saw the Catherine Institute on the Fontanka, also by Quarenghi, which has a similar central portico. But the effect over the wide Neva is entirely different. If you recall, the Catherine Institute portico was used to complete the vista down Rakov Street, which begins on the other side of the river—the Fontanka is that narrow. Here, Quarenghi's classical-style

building is one of a row that appears diminished by the water.

Next door on the right is the first museum in Russia, Peter the Great's **Kunstkamera** (1718–34) by Georg Mattarnovi, Mikhail Zemtsov, and G. Chiaveri. The striped facade anticipates the ornate surface decoration that would encrust baroque buildings of a few years later, of which the Winter Palace is the classic example. The Kunstkamera's tower (used as an observatory in Peter's day) hearkens back to the octagonal shapes of Moscow Baroque, making for a lovely amalgam of Old Russian and new Western motifs. It is here Peter gathered his collection of "monsters and oddities" (skeletons of extinct creatures; preserved specimens of deformed animals,

207

birds, and human beings; and astronomical and technical gear) for public display. The building now houses the **Museum of Anthropology and Ethnography**, which is open every day from 11:00 A.M. to 6:00 P.M. except Friday and Saturday.

As your gaze sweeps to the right, it breaks against the edge of Vasilievsky Island, where two strange-looking columns jut up against the sky. These are the **Rostral Columns** (1805–1810) by Thomas de Thomon, which served as port beacons (their peaks still torch with gas during city celebrations). The dark shapes jutting off the red pillars represent the bows of defeated ships, while Russia's great rivers (the Volga, Dnieper, Volkhov, and Neva) are personified in sculpture at the bases. It is hard to imagine a more perfect fusion of decoration, allegory, and utility. As sculpture, de Thomon's columns rank with the *Bronze Horseman* as one of the major works of the late eighteenth and early nineteenth centuries. Perhaps in utter strangeness the columns even surpass the equestrian monument, which is so squarely in the Western tradition.

Across the narrow spit of water over which the Rostral Columns flared are the brick bastions of the **Peter Paul Fortress**, surmounted by the golden spire and ribbed cupola of its cathedral. The fortress occupies almost all of **Hare Island** (Zaichiy Ostrov), which clearly commands the course of the Neva. It is here that St. Petersburg was founded, and from this point that it spread out to both banks of the Neva and the adjacent Vasilievsky Island.

In Walks 5 and 6 we looked at Petersburg's ensembles, vistas, and parks. Yet the view here is so encompassing that no single such term can be used. Palace, fortress, and cathedral—each unlike the other—are joined by the expanse of water and sky. Leningrad is among the most embellished of cities, but its receptivity to terrain and atmosphere gives its decoration a vivid life.

Now walk the Admiralty Embankment to your right until you reach the palace bridge crossing the Neva. Take note of the **second Admiralty pavilion**, which is identical to the one adjacent to the Senate Square. The buildings inset between the two were built in the late nineteenth century after the wharfs lying here were torn down.

At the entrance to the Palace Bridge, make a right into the grassy plaza. To the right (with your back to the river) is a facade of the **Admiralty**, duplicating the one that overlooks the Senate Square. Now is the moment to walk the main facade of the Admiralty, if you have extra time.

To the left is the **Winter Palace** (1754–62) by Bartolomeo Rastrelli, primary residence of the Russian monarchs from the eighteenth century until the February Revolution in 1917. Tickets to the palace, whose **Hermitage** is one of the greatest art museums in the world, are available in the summer at a kiosk on this side, usually notable for its long line. From fall through spring, tickets are available inside the entrance to the northern facade overlooking the Neva. Hours are 10:30 A.M. to 6:00 P.M. (last entry at 5:00) every day except Monday. If you are on your own you are best off getting tickets in the morning, since they usually sell out early in the day.

Rastrelli's palace is the example par excellence of Russian Baroque, in which a severe underlying order animates a surface encrusted with architectural details, in this case highlighted with white and gold. Unlike buildings of the later classical period, your attention is not drawn to refined proportions and smooth walls. Instead you lose yourself in tiny, worked-over portions of the facade.

The Winter Palace is the crowning architectural achievement of Empress Elizabeth's reign of 1741–61; ironically, Rastrelli's creation was finished after she died and Peter III was the first emperor to take up residence here. His reign lasted only a few months before he was deposed by his wife, Catherine the Great, whose architectural taste was more restrained. Thus one of the finest examples of Russian Baroque was also one of the last.

Do not confuse Russian Baroque with Moscow Baroque. The two styles are close in chronology but quite different in appearance. Russian Baroque is typical of mid-eighteenth-century Petersburg, and was applied almost exclusively to palaces, while Moscow Baroque was the exotic style favored in Moscow churches at the end of the seventeenth century.

Rastrelli was Russian Baroque's equivalent of the classical age's Carlo Rossi. In fact, if you leave Leningrad with the names of only two architects in memory they should be Rastrelli and Rossi. Strangely, their biographies parallel somewhat: both were Italian; both had parents who found work in Russia as artists, Rastrelli's father as a sculptor and Rossi's mother as a ballerina; and both learned to speak Russian well.

Whatever the similarities in background, their architectural styles are entirely different. Rastrelli did not think in terms of ensembles. He wanted to build the most compelling image of regal power and comfort that he could. His Winter Palace was designed to stand alone at the center of the city, a rival to the haughty Neva, and a message to the condescending monarchs of the West.

Walk into the huge **Palace Square** (Dvortsovaya Ploshad'), which opens up straight ahead and to the left. When the palace was completed the other buildings that now hem in the square did not exist. In fact the area was cluttered with bricks, lumber, and the debris of building, topped off by a mountain of public trash, a pile so enormous that it was impossible to cross from one side of the square to the other. Peter III agreed to the suggestion that the trash be offered to the public, and watched fascinated from the windows of the Winter Palace as thousands of his subjects descended on the square and stripped it bare in hours.

In a sense it is improper to use the word *square* in referring to that period. The **General Staff Headquarters** (1819–29) by Carlo Rossi directly across from the Winter Palace had not been built. Peter III would have had an open view to the Moika River, which flows on the opposite side of the staff building. Even the Admiralty to the right did not exist in its current form, and most of its perimeter consisted of bastions and palisades.

We mention all of this to emphasize just how much this region was transformed by the classical conception of ensemble. Notice the grand deference with which Rossi's massive building bows away from the Winter Palace opposite. It is a tribute to Rossi that the Winter Palace joins the ensemble without any loss to its dignity, almost as if Rastrelli's conception required this completion. The spareness of Rossi's facade flatters the Winter Palace, like a modestly dressed beauty curtseying to an older woman decked with jewels.

The General Staff Headquarters housed the Ministries of War, Foreign Affairs, and Finance—in other words, a good portion of the government bureaucracy in Petersburg. The building's center is marked by a **Triumphal Arch** celebrating the defeat of Napoleon. Above the arch a bronze Victory rides in a chariot pulled by six horses, by sculptors Pimenov and Demut Malinovsky. As legend has it, in the 1930s one of the horses was stolen, but the theft went unnoticed for months until some tourists corrected a guide's description of the sculpture. Investigators were able to recover the stolen horse and return it to duty.

No ensemble is complete without its particular vista (as we explained in Walk 5), but this one should come as a surprise. Walk through the Triumphal Archway in the General Staff Headquarters to the second arch, and turn back to face the Winter Palace. The central portion of the palace facade is beautifully framed by the first arch, with the granite Column of Alexander marking dead center.

Triumphal arch through the General Staff
Headquarters

You have no doubt noticed that the second archway curves once you enter the passage, in a manner not visible from the square. Rossi contrived this sleight to bring the passageway out perpendicular to Nevsky Prospect which lies just beyond. It is a twisting of form that ensures the illusion of perfect order, somewhat reminiscent of the "misplaced" colonnade we discovered at the Kazan Cathedral in Walk 5.

Return now to the center of the Palace Square and the **Column of Alexander** (1829–34), designed by Auguste Montferrand (also responsible for St. Isaac's and the monument to Nicholas I that began this walk). Like the Triumphal Arch, the column celebrates the defeat of Napoleon. The granite was quarried out of a cliff on the Gulf of Finland before it was floated by special barge to the capital. Konstantin Stanislavsky wrote that his grandfather was responsible for the transport of the 600-ton stone, and chose to brave a storm at sea rather than risk breaking Nicholas I's deadline for delivery. The angel at the top is by the sculptor Boris Orlovsky, and is said to symbolize the peaceful order in Europe following the Congress of Vienna.

On your right (as you face the Winter Palace), completing this side of the Palace Square, is the **Guards Headquarters** (1840), by A. Bryullov. The building is often praised for not intruding on the dialogue between the Winter Palace and the General Staff Headquarters, for resting almost unnoticed at the eastern edge of the square.

We leave the square by walking down the right side of this building and onto the bridge just beyond it. It is startling how quickly the scene changes. From Leningrad's grandest square we enter one of the most intimate quarters of the city, where pastel-colored buildings and extravagant ironwork reflect in narrow, arabesquing waterways. This is the Petersburg of Pushkin's day: from this **Pevchesky Most** (Singing Bridge) we have views in both directions similar to what he would have seen in the 1830s.

It is not the bridge that sings, but it often seems so when the Leningrad State Chorus is rehearsing with open windows at the **Choir Chapel**, the yellow building set back behind the magnificent grille at #20 directly across the river. Prior to the Revolution back to the eighteenth century, the chapel (reconstructed 1888–89) housed the Petersburg Chorus, and has numbered great composers among its directors, including Bortnyansky and Glinka. From the bridge look back over your shoulder for a view that sweeps across the Palace Square all the way to the Admiralty.

On a more prosaic note, clean public toilets for both men and women are available (10-kopeck charge) on the Palace Square side of the river at **#37**.

Cross the Singing Bridge to the opposite side of the Moika, and walk to the left along the embankment of the river. Just ahead, intersecting the Moika on your left is the **Little Winter Canal (Zimnaya Kanavka)**, which passes under a yellow covered bridge and into the Neva, visible beyond. This Italianate bridge connects the Old Hermitage with the Hermitage Theater, both of which were additions to the Winter Palace. The Little Winter Canal got its name from this covered bridge, which formerly housed a winter garden. We will walk down this canal shortly, after crossing the next bridge over the Moika and doubling back.

Just beyond this picturesque intersection of waterways (as we continue walking to the left) lies the building (**#12**) in which Pushkin lived the last four months of his life. His apartment has been resurrected as a museum (which you enter through the courtyard), fascinating both as literary history and as an evocation of the life-style of early nineteenth-century gentry. It is open every day except Tuesday, and the last Friday of each month, from 10:30 A.M. to 5:30 P.M. with the last entry at 4:30 P.M.. We highly recommend a visit, and English language tours are available.

Pushkin attracts fascination not simply because he

was a great poet but because his life seems emblematic of the age. To read his biography is to see Russia's contradictions laid bare. Judging from the apartment, the poet led a life in enviably decorous surroundings, with fine furniture, a good library, and a view of one of the loveliest streets in the world. His presence at virtually every court ball was required, and one may say without exaggeration that his wife, Natasha, was regarded as the most beautiful woman in St. Petersburg. Her appearance, however, was not matched by intellect. "No illuminating statements of Natasha's, no expression of fine feeling, no indication of refined taste have survived. She was simply a beautiful doll," wrote one of Pushkin's biographers.

Yet he loved her, just as he loved Petersburg's sensual surface, echoed in the gleam and rhythm of his untranslatable rhymes, rendered here in prose:

> "I love your severe, graceful appearance, the Neva's majestic current, the granite of her banks, the tracery of your cast-iron railings, the transparent twilight, the moonless gleam of your still nights. . . . The Admiralty spire is bright, and dawn hastens to succeed sunset, not letting the night's darkness rise to the golden heavens and leaving a bare half-hour for the night. I love the still air and the frost of your severe winter, the sleighs racing on the banks of the wide Neva. . . ."

Like Petersburg, Natasha was a paragon of physical beauty, hence Pushkin's need and his tragedy.

Although she was physically loyal to her husband, Natasha enjoyed flirting and inflamed many eager suitors indifferent to her marital state. In a bitter letter to a friend Pushkin once noted: "The Czar, like any officer, runs after my wife: several times in the mornings he has deliberately ridden past her window, and at evening during the balls he asks why she has her blinds lowered."

It is important to recall that Pushkin was a man under suspicion. As we described in Walk 4, he had been a friend of many of the Decembrists and had narrowly escaped arrest after the failed revolt. For propaganda reasons the czar chose to rehabilitate the popular poet, but at the same time he ensured that Pushkin's life was a torment. The secret police vigilantly watched him, and Nicholas interfered with Pushkin's publishing plans, thus further miring him in debt. The only reason Pushkin could afford this apartment was that the building owners, the Count Volkonsky family (whose scion was living in exile in Siberia for collaborating with the Decembrists), had let him have it inexpensively. The poet longed to leave Petersburg to retire to the country where he could begin to restore his finances and recover peace of mind. But Natasha was a creature of the ballroom and was happy only in the giddy embrace of waltzes and new gowns.

Her most persistent wooer was not the czar but the Baron George d'Anthes, a French adventurer who had won a commission in the Horse Guards through the influence of the Dutch minister, who had adopted the young man as his son. D'Anthes was tall, blond, and well built, the most handsome officer in a regiment of dashing lads. His courting was so blatant and rude that Pushkin had no choice but to challenge him to a duel. Both were eager to fight, but their seconds managed to get d'Anthes to agree to an astonishing solution: he would marry Natasha's sister, Ekaterina (who was madly in love with him), the implication being that he had been courting her all along, and not the poet's wife. The match amazed the capital, and even the empress expressed puzzled amusement.

No sooner had d'Anthes become a relation of Pushkin's than he renewed his efforts to bed Natasha. Pushkin forbade entrance to his home, but the officer insistently attended every function at which Natasha was expected. He pleaded for a private meeting and spoke to her of his passion. Natasha carefully related to her husband each step of d'Anthes's campaign, all the while doing little to repel him.

Pushkin finally had had enough. He addressed a letter to the Dutch minister that allowed satisfaction only in blood. "You, the representative of a crowned head, you have been as a father the pimp to your son. . . . Like an obscene old man, you have lain in wait for my wife in every corner to tell her of the love of your bastard, or so he is called; and when, ill with syphilis, he was obliged to remain at home, you said that he was dying from love of her; you muttered to her: Give me back my son."

D'Anthes made the challenge for his father, and Pushkin carefully kept the duel a secret from his friends, terrified that they might contrive some way to prevent it, as they had the last time. On January 27, 1837, in a snowy meadow outside of Petersburg he took a bullet in the abdomen, and in turn hit d'Anthes in the arm. Two days later, surrounded by friends, Pushkin died on the divan in the library of his apartment.

Nicholas persecuted Pushkin even in death and refused him a public funeral. The announced date of the service at St. Isaac's Cathedral was changed in secret to a midnight service at another church. Even so, large crowds appeared including much of the diplomatic corps, which reported on the funeral as if it had been an antigovernment demonstration. Many Russians held Nicholas indirectly responsible for the death of their greatest poet. Natasha, however, was well taken care of. Nicholas paid all of Pushkin's debts, provided her with a pension, and subsequently arranged a favorable marriage for her. Natasha's sister, Ekaterina, lived the rest of her life with d'Anthes, who moved on to Vienna where he made a good career. Natasha and Ekaterina were ideally adapted to the iron age of Nicholas, in which beauty thrived only so long as it was separated from conscience.

On the Little Winter Canal looking toward the Moika River

Simply to take in more of the color of the Moika, we suggest walking on to the **Large Stable Bridge (Bolshoi Konyushenniy Most)** visible not far ahead. It was built in 1818 and takes its name from the large building with a curving colonnade on the right, which was the Department of Stables, built by Vladimir Stasov in 1817–23.

Cross over to the other side of the Moika (the French and Japanese flags mark their consulates) and return back the way we came until you reach the Winter Canal. Facing us at the corner of the Winter Canal and the Moika is a lovely green building (**#35**) dating from 1800 in Empire style.

Now make a right and begin to stroll the short length of the Little Winter Canal. The first intersection we reach is with Khalturin (formerly Millionaires') Street. On the left is the **New Hermitage** (1839–52) by Leo Von Klenze, whose portico is supported by ten massively muscled Atlantes in dark granite (carved by A. Terebenev in 1840–48). This was the first building in Russia built specifically for use as a museum. Be sure to look also to your right. Millionaires' Street was one of the most prestigious addresses of the pre-Revolutionary period. Then take a moment to look back toward the Moika from the middle of the Khalturin Street bridge crossing the Little Winter Canal.

Just ahead to the left of the covered footbridge is the **Small Hermitage** (1764–1775) built by Vallin de la Mothe on orders of Catherine the Great to house her growing art collection, much of which can still be seen. Be absolutely sure not to leave Leningrad without having visited the Winter Palace and Hermitage complex. To the right of the covered bridge is evidence of Catherine's love of the stage, the **Hermitage Theater** (1783–87), built by Giacomo Quarenghi on her orders. The auditorium is still used for lectures and debates. The main facades of both of these buildings front the Neva, and it is from the Palace Embankment that they should really be studied.

So pass under the bridge and enter a whole new world, the vast space of the Neva all over again. We hope that by now you have begun to appreciate these transitions, from intimate spaces to grand ceremony, or from artifice to the open sky. The view we have from here would be difficult to appreciate fully without knowing the building blocks of which Leningrad is made: ensembles, vistas, columns, orders, parks, wrought iron, canals, and the grand Neva herself—all held together under the pearly sky of the north.

It remains only for us to lead you to a café where you can rest after this long walk. We suggest the café belonging to the **House of Scholars** at Palace Embankment (Dvortsovaya Naberezhnaya) #26, which is less than 100 feet to the right as you face the Neva. The entrance is at the far corner of the building, and the café serves from 11:00 A.M. until 4:00 P.M. (despite the sign which says until 5:00) every day. The interior decoration, in a style combining neo-Russian and beaux arts motifs, is original and dates from the 1880s. Pay special attention to the carved wood paneling and tile fireplace inside. You should be able to order pastries, sandwiches, tea, and sometimes wine or champagne. Just try your luck and see what they have.

One final suggestion. If you have the energy after the

café, try walking across the Palace Bridge (which begins at the Winter Palace). From the middle of the bridge, you will have a panoramic view of the entire left bank, so much of which we have explored. The bridge leads directly to the Strelka (Spit) of Vasilievsky Island, lorded over by the smoky-red Rostral Columns and the columned Stock Market (now the Naval Museum), all designed by Thomas de Thomon in 1805–1810. The grassy plaza at the Neva's edge, the farthest point of the Strelka, offers a good place to meditate on Leningrad's refinement, alive in all directions in a gray expanse of water and sky.

Useful Addresses and Telephone Numbers

Emergency (throughout the USSR)

Fire	01
Police	02
Ambulance	03

Moscow

American Express
21a Sadovaya Kudrinskaya
Tel. 254-4305; 254-4495

Intourist Headquarters
Mokhovaya (formerly Prospect Marksa) 16
Tel. 203-6962

Airlines

Aeroflot Offices
International Inquiries: 245-0002

Ulitsa Dobryninskaya 2
Tel. 238-7786

Mezhdunarodnaya 2
Tel. 253-8313

Ulitsa Petrovka 15
Tel. 928-8791

Cosmos Hotel
Tel. 215-3480

Rossiya Hotel
Tel. 298-1123

Ukraina Hotel
Tel. 243-3230

Air France
Ulitsa Dobryninskaya 7
Tel. 237-2325; 237-3344
At Sheremetevo 2 Airport: 578-2757

Alitalia
Ulitsa Pushechnaya 7
Tel. 928-2166
At Sheremetevo 2: 578-2767

Austrian Airlines
Krasnopresnenskaya Naberezhnaya 12, 18th floor
Tel. 253-1670/71

British Airways
Krasnopresnenskaya Naberezhnaya 12, 19th floor
Tel. 253-2481
Flight Information: 578-2936
At Sheremetevo 2: 578-2923

Japan Air Lines
Kuznetsky Most 3
Tel. 921-6448
At Sheremetevo 2: 578-2942/48

KLM
Krasnopresnenskaya Naberezhnaya 12, 13th floor
Tel. 253-2150/51
At Sheremetevo 2: 578-2762

Lufthansa
Kuznetsky Most 3
Tel. 923-0488
Flight Information: 921-9293
At Sheremetevo 2: 578-3151

Pan American
Krasnopresnenskaya Naberezhnaya 12, 11th floor
Tel. 253-2658/59
At American Embassy: 253-9871 (mornings)
At Sheremetevo 2: 578-2737

SAS
Kuznetsky Most 3
Tel. 925-4787
At Sheremetevo 2: 578-2727

Swissair
Krasnopresnenskaya Naberezhnaya 12, 20th floor
Tel. 253-8988; 253-1859/60
At Sheremetevo 2: 578-2740

Addresses and Telephone Numbers

Embassies

Australia
Kropotkinsky Pereulok 13
Tel. 246-5012

Canada
Starokonyushenny Pereulok 23
Tel. 241-5070; 241-4407

India
Ulitsa Obukha 6-8
Tel. 297-0820

Ireland
Grokholsky Pereulok 5
Tel. 288-4101; 288-4192

New Zealand
Ulitsa Vorovskogo 44
Tel. 290-3485; 290-1277

Pakistan
Ulitsa Sadovaya Kudrinskaya 17
Tel. 250-3991; 254-9791

United Kingdom
Naberezhnaya Morisa Toreza 14
Tel. 231-8511/12

United States
Novinsky Bulvar (formerly Ulitsa Tchaikovskogo) 19/23
Tel. 252-2451/59

Addresses and Telephone Numbers

Hospitals

For ambulance dial 03

Diplomatic and Foreigners' Polyclinics

> 4th Dobryinsky Pereulok 4
> Tel. 237-5933; 237-8338

> Ulitsa Gertsena 12
> Tel. 229-7323; 229-0382

Botkin Hospital
2nd Botkinsky Proezd 5
Tel. 255-0015; 256-0033

French-Soviet Joint Venture Clinic
Parkovaya Ulitsa 15 (2-4)
Tel. 465-8456; 464-4054

International Health Care (Private Clinic)
Gruzinsky Pereulok 3, Bldg. 2
Tel. 253-0703; 253-0704

Tourists' Clinic
Gruzinsky Proezd 2
Tel. 254-4396

Legal Counsel and Registration

Intercollegia (for counsel)
Tverskaya Ulitsa (formerly Gorkogo) 5
Tel. 203-5828

Marriage Palace
Ulitsa Griboyedova 10
Tel. 924-3188

Moscow Registry Office (Marriage, Birth, Death)
Tel. 924-1561

UVIR (Department of Visas and Registration)
Kolpachny Pereulok 10
Tel. 924-9349

Leningrad

American Express
c/o Pan American Airways
Ulitsa Gertsena 36
Tel. 311-5215
Hours Monday–Friday 9:00–5:00

Intourist Headquarters
Isaakievskaya Ploshad' (St. Isaac's Square) 11
Tel. 214-6420

United States Consulate General
Ulitsa Petra Lavrova 15
Tel. 274-8235

Airlines

Aeroflot
Nevsky Prospect 7-9
Tel. 211-7980

British Airways
c/o Pan American Airways
Ulitsa Gertsena 36
Tel. 311-5819/20/22

Finnair
Ulitsa Gogolya 19
Tel. 315-9736; 312-8987

KLM
Pulkovo Airport
Tel. 122-1981

Pan American
Ulitsa Gertsena 36
Tel. 311-5819/20/22
(Hours Monday–Friday 9:00–5:00)

Hospitals

Eye Clinic
Mokhovaya Ulitsa 38
Tel. 273-1631

Ear, Nose, and Throat Clinic
Bronnitskaya Ulitsa 9
Tel. 292-2841

For serious illnesses, evacuation to Helsinki would be a good idea. Here are some clinic names and addresses:

Kätilöopisto (Maternity)
Sofianlehdenk 5
Tel. 790-411

Deaconess Medical Center
Alppikatu 2
Tel. 750-161

Addresses and Telephone Numbers

Dextra Medical Center
Raumantie 1a
Tel. 550-025

Halsingin Lääkärikeskus
Mannerheimintie 12
Tel. 646-411

Restaurants
and Cafés

Moscow

Atrium, 44 Leninsky Prospect, tel. 137-3008. A trendy café with well-done post-modern decor, the Atrium could pass easily for the latest hot spot in TriBeCa, Manhattan. The food is traditional and well prepared. Convenient only if you have a car at your disposal.

Glazur, 12 Smolensky Bulvar, tel. 248-4438. This restaurant, located in a small pink building two blocks from the Foreign Ministry on the Garden Ring Road, is a good place to go for a classically Russian meal. Beer and foreign wines are also available, and it has a bakery on the ground floor. This restaurant is several long blocks from the Arbat, where it intersects the Garden Ring. Use the Smolenskaya metro stop to get there.

Kropotkinskoye Café, 36 Prechistenka (formerly Kropotkinskaya) Street, tel. 201-7500. Moscow's first cooperative café, the Kropotkinskoye is also among the best, and sometimes features live classical piano and violin music. The restaurant's *zakuski* (appetizers) are good, but it is in its entrees that it has made its mark. There are separate ruble and hard-currency rooms. The restaurant was named for its street, which has recently had its traditional name restored by the Moscow City Soviet. It remains to be seen whether the restaurant's name will change as well. It is near the beginning of Walk 4.

Café Margarita, 28 Malaya Bronnaya, tel. 299-6539. This café is named for the heroine of Mikhail Bulgakov's novel, *Master and Margarita*, whose beginning is set right across the street at the Patriarch Ponds (formerly Pioneers' Ponds). Both the literary connection and the tasty pastries make the tiny café popular with American students of Russian literature, many of whom make a pilgrimage to the ponds. The café also has the advantage of being in one of Moscow's most charming neighborhoods. It is about a fifteen-minute walk from the Ryabushinsky Mansion, which concludes Walk 4.

Moskovskiye Zori, 11 Kozihinsky Maly Pereulok, tel. 299-5725. The restaurant (its name means "Moscow Dawns") takes rubles only and is one of our favorites on several counts: atmosphere, service, food, and price. The stained pine-plank walls are covered with old woodcuts, engravings, and watercolors of Moscow. There is also an outdoor section for tea and desserts, with tables and chairs fashioned out of logs, and a sandbox for children. The fare is simple but carefully prepared (usually a single entree, often pork accompanied by vegetables, is offered); the staff is exceptionally polite; the desserts are terrific; and foreigners are rarely in evidence. Perhaps best of all, wallet and palate will find the meal equally congenial. Near Café Margarita, it is also about a fifteen-minute walk from the end of Walk 4.

Natsional, 1 Tverskaya (formerly Gorky) Street in the art nouveau style National Hotel, tel. 203-5595. The hotel is directly across the Mokhovaya (formerly Prospect Marksa) from Red Square. An illustrious line of visitors to the Soviet Union has stayed in this hotel (built in 1903) over the decades since the Revolution, and it figures in many memoirs. The restaurant on the second floor has a postcard-worthy view of the Kremlin and Red Square, although the expensive cuisine does not quite match up. There is also a separate bar on the second floor open late at night for hard currency only. Its clientele includes beautiful and unattached ladies many might find a bit brazen. The Natsional is state run. Its location makes it convenient to Walks 1 and 2.

Praga, 2 Arbat, tel. 290-6171. This huge restaurant, with many separate floors, dining halls, and balconies, is one of the largest in Moscow and boasts elegant interiors and live entertainment as well as views. Despite the name (Prague), it offers only a few Czech dishes in addition to the rather bland Russian fare. The Praga is state run. We pass it midway through Walk 4.

Sakura, 12 Krasnopresnenskaya Naberezhnaya, in the Mezhdunarodnaya Hotel, tel. 253-3894. Moscow does boast a Japanese restaurant with good sushi, very popular with visiting Japanese businessmen. It is expensive and payment is in hard currency only. The restaurant is located in the slick, modern Mezhdunarodnaya Hotel.

Skazka, 1 Tovarishchevsky Pereulok, tel. 271-0998. An evening at the Skazka (Fairy Tale) is about as expensive as a night of jazz in New York City but every bit as enjoyable. The paintings and carved furniture evoke a folk feeling, with cubist-style lamps that could have adorned an avant-garde café of 1915–16. Unless you specify otherwise when you make your reservation, you will be seated at a table set with *zakuski*. The meal will be accompanied by live entertainment that changes every twenty minutes; for example, banjo and guitar music, a lithe and scantily clad dancer, Cossack folk singers, and best of all, Gypsy musicians. The Skazka lies to the east of Kitai Gorod down toward the Moskva River. The Taganskaya metro stop on the Brown Circle Line is fairly close.

Slavyansky Bazaar, 13 Nikolskaya (formerly 25th of October) Street, tel. 921-1872. This is Kitai Gorod's most famous restaurant, and has been an institution since the early nineteenth century when it also served as a hotel. The hero of Chekhov's tragic story, "Lady with a Dog" had his assignations here, and the hotel restaurant was the favorite gathering place of Moscow's industrialists right up until the 1917 Revolution. The state-run restaurant can be noisy and the traditional Russian dishes rarely rise to excellence, but the restaurant is a piece of history. It is perfect for Walk 2, only a few steps to the right of the Old Printing House on Nikolskaya Street.

Stanislavskogo 2, 2 Ulitsa Stanislavskogo, tel. 291-8689. From the street this restaurant, with lovely lace curtains hiding the interior, is intriguing, and it is a pleasant stop if you can get a reservation. Stanislavskogo Street is named for dramatist Konstantin Stanislavsky. You might want to combine a meal at the restaurant with a visit to the Stanislavsky Museum at #7 Ulitsa Stanislavskogo, which is open 11:00 A.M. until 6:00 P.M. Thursday, Saturday, and Sunday; and 2:00 until 7:00 P.M. Wednesday and Friday. The restaurant is two blocks from the Ryabushinsky Mansion, which concludes Walk 4.

U Nikitskikh Vorot, Ulitsa Gertsena at Suvorovsky Bulvar, tel. 290-4825. Also about two blocks from the Ryabushinsky Mansion is this restaurant (its name means "At the Nikitski Gates," a reference to the passageway through the Byeli Gorod walls that were torn down in the early nineteenth century), which charges rubles only. The menu is simple and the prices are very moderate.

U Pirosmani, 4 Novodyevichi Proezd, tel. 247-1926. The restaurant has a lovely view of the spires, white parapets, and red brick walls of the Novodyevichi Convent. Inside, the walls are hung with strong, lurid portraits in the naive expressionist manner of Niko Pirosmani, Georgia's most famous modern painter, for whom the restaurant is named. The restaurant purveys spicy Georgian cuisine, including some of the best *zakuski* in Moscow, accompanied by tart wine perfectly suited to the food. The restaurant serves as an ideal conclusion to Walk 3.

Vareniki, at the corner of Ulitsa Paliashvili and Skatertny Pereulok. The flimsy exterior walls look inauspicious, but the interior is pleasantly decorated. *Vareniki* are a sort of cheese- or cabbage-filled dumpling, and the restaurant makes these a specialty, in addition to its soup and chicken dishes. You order at the counter and take a seat, where you will be served. The food is tasty, filling, caloric, and incredibly inexpensive. Two people can dine well for under 10 rubles. No reservations are necessary. We walk right past this one toward the end of Walk 4.

Leningrad

Admiralteisky, Ulitsa Gertsena 27. Inexpensive and cozy, with dim lighting and still-life paintings of food. Has long been known for well-prepared steaks. It is close to St. Isaac's Square and the beginning of Walk 7. If you feel hungry before beginning you can stop in for a quick meal. When the weather is good there are often tables set up on the street with a cart selling pastries. Rubles only. No reservations necessary.

Astoria Hotel Restaurant, Isaakiyevsky Ploshad' (St. Isaac's Square), tel. 219-1100. The hotel and its restaurant have reopened after a long renovation, and we can only hope that little has changed. Service was unobtrusive, polite, and frock-coated; dinner was served on real silver; wine in crystal; and digestion aided by a fine orchestra—you could have been in Petersburg of 150 years ago. The staff was far too well trained to give off the faintly criminal aura that mars many of Russia's better restaurants. In the evening the Astoria is expensive but worth it. Another tradition we hope they continue is the buffet hall for breakfast and lunch, notable both for its selection and reasonable price. Both ruble and hard-currency halls. This one is perfect for the beginning of Walk 7.

Aquarium (Ice Cream Café), near the beginning of Nevsky Prospect at the corner of Ulitsa Zhelyabova. This café, popular with students and young people, is nicknamed the "Frog Aquarium" because of the frogs in the decor. In addition to ice cream and desserts, champagne and liquor are served. Rubles only.

Evropeiskaya Hotel, Ulitsa Brodskogo 1/7, tel. 211-9149. This hotel is due to reopen imminently, after renovation. Leningrad has been washed with rumors that its grand baroque furniture has all disappeared into the maw of the black market. If that is true, it will be a loss to both atmosphere and comfort. The hotel had several restaurants including one on the roof with a winter garden. The food has always been good, if rarely outstanding. Rubles or hard currency.

Literaturnaya Café, Nevsky Prospect 18, tel. 310-2281. It is from here that Pushkin set out in 1837 to his fatal duel. In terms of atmosphere this is one of the best places in Leningrad, and the food, while not outstanding, is passable. Every night on the second floor is a literary or musical program. Entry into the restaurant is only with tickets that have to be bought ahead of time. Make your reservations early in the day to guarantee a table, and specify if you want to be on the second floor. Rubles only. Convenient to Walks 5 and 6.

Moskva Hotel, Ploshad' Aleksandra Nevskogo 2 (across from Lavra Alexandra Nevskogo), tel. 274-2051, 274-9115. This is one of those Intourist hotels with buffets on many of its floors that are open at hours when restaurant doors are jammed shut. It is particularly convenient as a conclusion to a visit to the Alexander Nevsky Lavra, one of Russia's major monastic centers, across Nevsky Prospect.

Na Fontanke, Naberezhnaya Reki Fontanka 77, tel. 311-4526. One of Leningrad's new cooperatives, it takes rubles only and has a very good reputation for food, atmosphere, and price.

Neva, Nevsky Prospect 44, tel. 311-3678. Beautifully renovated in modern style. Circular hall on two levels with dark stained wooden walls, and an orchestra and dance floor below. Imaginative lighting helps induce a feeling that each table is separate from others, even when they are fairly close together. Food rather standard but enjoyable. Rubles only. Very centrally located, again it is convenient to Walks 5 and 6.

Café Sever, next door to the Neva Restaurant at Nevsky Prospect 46. This café is famous for its ice cream and cakes, and is considered to have the best desserts in Leningrad. A grill bar offers heavier fare and liquor. There is a dance floor that sports a very young clientele. Rubles only.

Nevsky, Nevsky Prospect 71, above the entrance to the Mayakovskaya metro stop. It is five floors, each with a separate restaurant and bar. The most beautiful hall is on the fifth floor, and is decorated with a winter garden and a fountain. Adequate but uninspiring food. Popular for dancing and drinking, especially with out-of-town rubes from Central Asia and the Caucasus, who come here to spend after making a killing in the farmers' markets. Rubles or hard currency. Convenient to Walks 5 and 6.

Olympia Hotel Restaurant, Ploshad' Morskoi Slava 21, tel. 217-4051. Expensive, with a reputation for good food and service. Hard currency only.

Sadko, Ulitsa Brodskogo 1, at the corner of Nevsky Prospect. This restaurant is soon to reopen after renovation. If it follows the old formula it will have three halls: the first with a Russian folk orchestra, the second with a Gypsy ensemble, and the third with a variety show. Its grilled dishes, fish, fowl, and game were well prepared. Very expensive. Hard currency or rubles. Well located for Walk 5.

Schwabsky Domik, Krasnaya Gvardeiskaya 28-29, near the Narvskaya stop on the metro, tel. 528-2211. If Leningrad's examples of Hanseatic-style architecture inspire a craving for German cuisine this restaurant is the place to retire to. The product is authentic if expensive, with both ruble and hard-currency halls available.

Tête-à-Tête, Bolshoi Prospect 65, on the Petrogradskaya Storona (Petrograd Side), tel. 232-7548. As the name suggests, this new cooperative café is small and intimate. The food is very good and prices moderate.

Troika, Prospect Zagorodny 27, tel. 113-5343. This establishment offers what locals consider the best restaurant variety show in town. It attracts a colorful clientele that includes well-heeled black marketeers. Not the place to go if you are looking for a quiet evening, it can be a lot of fun in the right mood. The food is good and expensive. Hard currency only.

Volkhov, Liteiny Prospect 28, tel. 273-2262. A simple restaurant frequented by staff members from the American Consulate, and perhaps by the Leningrad KGB, whose headquarters is one block away. Traditional Russian food served in clay pots. Very inexpensive. Rubles only.

Shops

Moscow

Beriozkas and Hard-Currency Stores

Keep in mind that these stores accept only hard currency and credit cards. Although prices are marked in rubles, the conversion is calculated at the old, unfavorable rate of $1.62 to the ruble. However, for convenience these stores cannot be beat: they carry many items that are hard to find or altogether unavailable in ruble stores. Every major Intourist hotel has a Beriozka. Only the largest are listed below. For any items you hope to export, be sure to keep your receipts with you to prove to customs the location of your purchase.

Sadko (A joint-venture food store)
Bolshaya Dorogomilovskaya Ulitsa 16
Hours: Monday–Saturday, 10:00–2:00, 3:00–8:00.
You will see many familiar brands here in addition to perishable foods.

Stockmann's
Ulitsa Zatsepskiy Val 4/8
This unusually well-supplied grocery is a Finnish
venture. Be forewarned: they do not accept cash, only
credit cards.

Beriozka Bookstore
Kropotkinskaya Ulitsa 31
Hours: Monday–Saturday, 9:00–8:00.
Hard to find twentieth-century Russian classics (Akh-
matova, Mandelstam, Pasternak, Bulgakov, etc.) are
readily available here, as well as in some of the other
Beriozkas. These editions make perfect hostess gifts
if a Russian family invites you to dinner.

Mezhdunarodnaya Hotel-2
Krasnopresnenskaya Naberezhnaya 12
Beriozka hours: Monday–Saturday, 9:00–2:00, 3:00–
8:00.
The hotel's Beriozka is divided into areas for food,
electronics, clothing, jewelry and books, and other
items. In addition, the hotel has many Western bou-
tiques.

Rossiya Hotel
Varvarka (formerly Ulitsa Razina) 6
Hours: Daily, 9:00–8:00.
One of the largest Beriozkas in Moscow is housed on
the ground floor of the hotel on the side overlooking
the Moskva River. China, crystal, furs, liquor, books,
and more are all available.

Novodyevichi Convent
Opposite the Monastery
Hours: Monday–Saturday, 9:00–7:00.
Another of the best-stocked Beriozkas in Moscow.

Sovamico
Hotel Sovietskaya
32/2 Leningradsky Prospect
Hours: Monday–Saturday, 11:00–7:00.
For antiques and expensive bric-a-brac.

Vneshtorgbank Gold Shop
Ulitsa Pushkinskaya 9
Hours: Monday–Friday, 10:00–1:30, 2:30–5:00.
For gold, precious stones, jade, and jewelry.

Jewelry Salon
Grokholsky Pereulok 30
Hours: Monday–Friday, 9:00–6:00.

Commission Stores (Kommissioniy Magazini)

These are stores that sell second-hand items, sometimes including valuable antiques, paintings, jewelry, or electronic goods. You must be careful not to run afoul of customs in exporting purchases. Commission stores are typically open Monday through Saturday from 11:00 to 8:00.

Ulitsa Dimitrova 54/58
Tel. 238-9545
One of the largest. Samovars, china, crystal, and *objets* are among the items for sale.

Frunzenskaya Naberezhnaya 54
Boasts antiques, clocks, and mirrors.

Smolenskaya Naberezhnaya 5/13
Looking for a brushy impressionist-style landscape from the turn of the century? This gallery has some old paintings on consignment.

Tverskaya (formerly Gorkogo) Ulitsa 46
Tel. 251-6548
More *objets*, china, and crystal.

Arbat 32
You can try dropping in on your stroll down the
Arbat for more china and crystal.

Ruble Stores

The same concerns that apply to commission stores hold
here with older items. Otherwise, have fun.

Food Stores
As we have all heard on the news, Russians face many
shortages in their grocery stores. Except out of curiosity
there is little point in exploring the state-run gastronoms
and worsening the plight of locals.

You will, however, be welcomed into farmers' markets
where neither shortages nor price controls are in evidence. Many of the prices in fact are fixed artificially high,
a policy enforced by muscle, as Russian journalists working under cover have reported. Nevertheless, these markets are a godsend to foreigners in Moscow who have
ready access through them to fresh vegetables, cheese,
fruit, and meat. Most of these markets are open from 7:00
until 5:00 or 6:00 in the evening. Two of the best are:

Cheryomushkinsky Rynok
Lomonosovsky Prospect 3

Tsentralny Rynok
Tsvetnoi Bulvar 15

Other Stores
GUM (pronounced *Goom*)
Krasnaya Ploshad' 3
The State Department Store on Red Square is actually

a huge complex of stores connected by ramps and skylit corridors that replaced Moscow's old trading rows dating back to medieval days. If you want to get a feeling for Russian clothing, cutlery, fabrics, or just about anything else, browse through GUM and pop into the individual stores that strike your fancy. You are bound to find an unexpected bargain.

Detsky Mir (Children's World)
Mokhovaya (formerly Prospect Marksa) 2
Near GUM, this is the Soviet equivalent of Toys R Us. It is often crowded. Look carefully and you'll find a present for some kids back home. Wooden toys, or those that have a craft element to them are often particularly attractive.

Tsentralny Voyenniy Univermag (Central Military Department Store)
Vozdvizhenka (formerly Prospect Kalinina) 10
Ever wonder where all those Soviet army belts that were the rage several years ago came from? From here, although the store seems to have cracked down on the sale of some military clothing to foreigners.

Dom Farfor (House of China)
Leninsky Prospect 36
Worth a try, although the pickings are slimmer and slimmer.

Khozaistvenniy Magazin (Household Store)
There are many around the city, identified by the name above, which sell everything from hardware to kitchen implements. One of the largest is at Bolshaya Dorogomiloskaya 60.

Tkani (Fabrics)
There are many of these as well, identified by the word for "fabrics." Try them. You can point to the bolts

of fabric you'd like to examine. If you are planning new curtains, hold off until you've visited Russia. You won't believe the bargains.

Dom Tkani (House of Fabrics)
Leninsky Prospect 9

Khrustal (Crystal) Store
Tverskaya (formerly Gorkogo) Ulitsa 15
or Ulitsa Kirova 8/2

The best advice is simply to walk in if a store looks interesting. If you see something you like, buy it. Don't give someone else a chance.

Leningrad

Beriozkas

As in Moscow, most Intourist hotels have Beriozkas. Only the largest are listed below. Keep in mind that most close for lunch.

Ulitsa Gertsena 26

Nevsky Prospect 7/9

Pribaltiskaya Hotel (both sides)
Morskaya Naberezhnaya 9 and 15

Hotel Sovietskaya
Lermontovsky Prospect 43

Shops

Ruble Stores

Gostinniy Dvor
Nevsky Prospect 35
Hours: 10:00–9:00.
This is Leningrad's answer to GUM, a shopping arcade dating back to the eighteenth century. It's a very good place to begin if you want to see a whole range of Soviet stores in one location. It is also very close to the beginnings of Walks 5 and 6.

Passazh
Nevsky Prospect 48
Hours: Monday–Saturday, 10:00–9:00.
Women's goods from souvenirs to cosmetics, fabrics, clothes, furs, perfumes. It has a particularly good hat boutique.

Biryuza (Turquoise)
Nevsky 69; tel. 312-2176
Semi-precious stones and jewelry.

Farfor Khrustal (China Crystal)
Nevsky Prospect 64
or Nevsky 147

Lavka Khudozhnikov (Store of Artists)
Nevsky 8
Paintings, jewelry, and crafts by members of the Union of Artists.

Naslediya (Inheritance)
Nevsky 116; tel. 311-0690
Art gallery with contemporary paintings.

Podarki (Presents)
Nevsky 54
Cosmetics, leatherwork, silver plate, clothes, toys.

Polyarnaya Zvezda (Polar Star)
158 Nevsky
Semi-precious jewelry.

Samotsveta (Semi-Precious Stones)
Ulitsa Brodskogo 4; tel. 311-9157

Tkani (Fabrics)
Nevsky 32-34

Farmers' Markets

Nekrasovsky Rynok
Ulitsa Nekrasova 52

Vladimirsky Rynok
Right at the Vladimirskaya metro stop.

Museums

Moscow

Art Museums

Museums of the Moscow Kremlin
Hours: Daily 10:00–6:00 except Thursday
Tickets to the Kremlin Cathedrals are available in the Alexander Garden below the Trinity Gate. Tickets to the Armory and Diamond Fund must be purchased at the Intourist office at Tverskaya Ulitsa 3.

Tretyakov Gallery
Lavrushinsky Pereulok 10
The world-famous museum is closed for renovation until late 1991 or 1992. Ask the service bureau in your hotel for a status report. The Tretyakov has a modern extension on Krymsky Val across from Gorky Park.

Pushkin Museum of Art
Ulitsa Vokhonka 12
Closed Monday.

Hours: Tuesday–Saturday, 10:00–8:00; Sunday 10:00–6:00.
One of Moscow's great art museums.

Folk Arts Museum
Ulitsa Stanislavskogo 7
Closed Monday and the last day of each month.
Hours: Tuesday and Thursday, noon–8:00; Wednesday–Sunday, 10:00–5:00.

Shchusev Museum of Architecture
Vozdvizhenka (formerly Kalinina) 5
Hours: Daily 11:00–7:00 except Monday, Friday, and the last Thursday of each month.

Rublev Museum of Old Russian Art
Ploshad' Pryamikov 10
Although the work of Andrei Rublev, Russia's greatest icon painter, is not represented here, that of his contemporaries and students is. The museum has been under renovation; ask the service bureau in your hotel whether it has reopened.

Church Museums

Church of the Trinity in the Nikitnikis
Nikitnikov Pereulok 3
Hours: Daily 10:00–6:00 except Wednesday and Thursday, when hours are noon–8:00.

Church of Fili
Novozavodskaya Ulitsa 6
Closed from October through May 1.
Hours: Monday and Thursday, 1:00–8:00; Friday–Sunday, 11:00–6:00.

St. Basil's Cathedral Museum
Red Square

Hours: Daily 9:30–5:30 except Tuesdays. Last entry at 5:00 P.M.

Novodyevichi Convent
1 Novodyevichi Proezd
Hours: Daily 10:00–5:30 except Tuesdays and the last day of each month. From November 1 to April, closes at 5:00 P.M.

Kolomonskoye Museum and Cathedral
Proletarsky Prospect 31
Closed Monday and Tuesday.
Hours: September–April, 11:00–5:00; May–August, on Wednesday and Thursday 1:00–8:00 and on Friday–Sunday 11:00–5:00.
Even when the museum is closed, it is worth a trip just to get a look at one of Moscow's great "tent"-style churches.

Donskoy Monastery
Donskaya Ploshad' 1
Closed Monday, Friday, and the last Thursday of each month.
Hours: 10:00–6:00; 10:00–5:00 from October 1 through April.

Historical Museums

State Historical Museum
Red Square
Closed Tuesday and the last Monday of each month.
Hours: Wednesday 11:00–7:00; other days 10:00–6:00.

Central Lenin Museum
Ploshad' Revolutsii 2
Closed Monday and the last Tuesday of each month.
Hours: October–April, Tuesday–Thursday, 11:00–7:00;

Friday–Sunday, 10:00–6:30. May–September, Tuesday, Thursday, and Friday, 10:00–6:00; Wednesday, Saturday, and Sunday, 11:00–7:30

Central Museum of the Revolution
Tverskaya Ulitsa 21
Closed Monday.
Hours: Wednesday and Friday, 11:00–7:00; Tuesday, Thursday, Saturday, and Sunday, 10:00–6:00.

Sixteenth and Seventeenth Century Boyar Chambers
Varvarka (formerly Ulitsa Razina) 10
Closed Tuesday and the first Monday of each month.
Hours: Thursday–Monday, 10:00–6:00; Wednesday 11:00–7:00.
This museum is due to reopen imminently, and is dedicated to preserving a sense of how boyars lived.

Museum of the History of Moscow
Novaya Ploshad' 12
Hours: Wednesday and Friday, noon–8:00; Tuesday, Thursday, Saturday, and Sunday, 10:00–6:00.

Panorama of the Battle of Borodino
38 Kutuzovsky Prospect 38
Closed Friday and the last Thursday of each month.
Hours: 10:30–4:00.
The 115-meter-long (450 feet) painting by Franz Roubaud renders the cataclysmic battle of Napoleon's drive into Russia.

Theatrical, Musical, and Literary Museums

Bakhrushin Theatrical Museum
31/12 Ulitsa Bakhrushina
Closed Tuesday and the last Monday of each month.

Hours: Wednesday and Friday, 1:00–8:00; Monday, Thursday, Saturday, and Sunday, noon–7:00.

Anton Chekhov House Museum
Sadovaya Kudrinskaya 6
Closed Monday and the last day of each month.
Hours: Tuesday, Thursday, Saturday, and Sunday, 11:00–6:00; Wednesday and Friday, 2:00–8:30.

Dostoyevsky Apartment Museum
Ulitsa Dostoyevskogo 2
Closed Monday, Tuesday, and the last day of each month.
Hours: Thursday, Saturday, and Sunday, 11:00–6:00; Wednesday and Friday, 2:00–9:00.
Dostoyevsky's residence (1823–1837) now houses memorabilia and exhibitions in his honor.

Glinka Museum
Ulitsa Fadeyeva 4
Closed Monday and the last day of each month.
Hours: Tuesday and Thursday, 2:00–8:00; Wednesday, Friday, Saturday, and Sunday, 10:00–6:00.
This museum is dedicated not simply to Glinka, but to Russian composers of the nineteenth century.

Maksim Gorky Museum
Ulitsa Vorovskogo 25a
Closed Monday, Tuesday, and the last Friday of each month.
Hours: Wednesday and Friday, noon–8:00; Thursday, Saturday, and Sunday, 10:00–5:45.

Maksim Gorky House Museum (Ryabushinsky Mansion)
Ulitsa Kachalova 6/2
Closed Monday and Tuesday.
Hours: Wednesday and Friday, noon–8:00; Thursday, Saturday, and Sunday, 10:00–5:45.

Lermontov House Museum
Malaya Molchanovka Ulitsa 2
Closed Monday, Tuesday, and the last day of each month.
Hours: Wednesday and Friday, 2:00–9:00; Thursday, Saturday, and Sunday, 11:00–6:00.

Literature Museum
Petrovka 28
Closed Monday and the last day of each month.
Hours: Tuesday, Thursday, Saturday, and Sunday, 11:00–6:00; Wednesday and Friday, 2:00–9:00.

Mayakovsky Museum
Proezd Serova 3/6
Closed: Wednesday.
Hours: Tuesday, Friday, Saturday, and Sunday, 10:00–6:00; Monday and Thursday, noon–8:00.

Pushkin Museum
Prechistenka (formerly Kropotkinskaya) 12/2
Closed Monday and the last Friday of each month.
Hours: Tuesday, Wednesday, Thursday, and Friday, noon–8:00; Saturday and Sunday, 10:00–6:00.

Pushkin Apartment Museum
Arbat 53
Closed Monday, Tuesday, and the last Friday of each month.
Hours: Wednesday, Thursday, and Friday, noon–6:00; Saturday and Sunday, 11:00–5:00.

Stanislavsky House Museum
Ulitsa Stanislavskogo 6
Closed Monday, Tuesday, and the last Thursday of each month.
Hours: Wednesday and Friday, 2:00–9:00; Thursday, Saturday, and Sunday, 11:00–6:00.

Museums

Lev Tolstoy Museum
Prechistenka (formerly Kropotkinskaya) 11
Closed Monday and the last Friday of each month.
Hours: Tuesday, Thursday, Saturday, and Sunday, 11:00–7:00; Wednesday and Friday, noon–8:00.

Lev Tolstoy Estate Museum
Ulitsa Lva Tolstogo 21
Closed Monday and the last Friday of each month.
Hours: April–September, 10:00–5:00; October–March, 10:00-4:00.

Vasnetsov House Museum
Pereulok Vasnetsova 13
Hours: Wednesday and Friday, 12:00–7:00; Thursday, Saturday, and Sunday, 10:00–5:00.

Scientific Museums

Anthropology Museum
Mokhovaya (formerly Prospect Marksa) 18

Charles Darwin Museum
Malaya Pirogovskaya Ulitsa 1
Closed Saturday and Sunday.
Hours: Monday–Friday, 10:00–5:00.

Exhibition of Economic Achievements (VDNKh)
This huge park with its own metro stop has a series of pavilions with exhibits about Soviet scientific achievements.
Hours: Daily 10:00–9:00 (in winter closes at 6:00).

Memorial Museum of Cosmonauts
Ulitsa Kosmonavtov (near VDNKh)

Closed Monday.
Hours: Tuesday–Thursday, noon–8:00; Friday–Sunday, 11:00–5:30.

Mineralogical Museum
Leninsky Prospect 18
Closed Monday, Wednesday, Friday, and Saturday.
Hours: Tuesday, Thursday, and Sunday, 11:00–5:00.

Planetarium
Sadovaya Kudrinskaya 5
Closed Tuesday.
Hours: Monday and Wednesday–Saturday, 1:00–6:00; Sunday, 10:00–6:00.

Zoological Museum
Ulitsa Gertsena 6
Closed Monday and the last Tuesday of each month.
Hours: Tuesday, Thursday, Saturday, and Sunday, 10:00–5:00; Wednesday and Friday, noon–8:00.

Leningrad

Art Museums

Hermitage and Winter Palace
Dvortsovaya Naberezhnaya 34
Closed Monday.
Hours: Spring and summer 9:30–4:30; fall and winter 10:30–6:30.

State Russian Museum
Inzhinirnaya Ulitsa 4
Closed Tuesday.
Hours: 11:00–6:00.

Historical and Palace Museums

Domik (Little House) of Peter I
Petrovskaya Naberezhnaya 6
Closed Tuesday and the last Monday of each month.
Hours: 11:00–7:00.

Central Lenin Museum
Ulitsa Khalturina 5/1
Closed Wednesday.
Hours: 10:30–7:00.

The Cruiser Aurora
Petrogradskaya Naberezhnaya 4
Closed Friday.
Hours: 10:30–4:30.

Great October Revolution Museum
Ulitsa Kuibysheva 4
Closed Thursday.
Hours: Monday and Friday, noon–7:00; other days
noon–6:00.

Menshikov Palace
Universitetskaya Naberezhnaya 15
Closed Monday.
Hours: 10:30–4:30.

Naval Museum (in the former Stock Exchange)
Pushkinskaya Ploshad' 4
Closed Monday and Tuesday.
Hours: 10:30–4:30.

Peter Paul Fortress
On Zaichy (Rabbit) Island
Closed Wednesday and the last Tuesday of each month.
Hours: 11:00–6:00.

St. Isaac's Cathedral
Closed Wednesday.
Hours: 11:00–5:00 (Tuesdays until 4:00).

Summer Palace of Peter I
Naberezhnaya Kutuzova side of the Summer Garden
Closed November 11–April 30, as well as Tuesdays.
Hours: noon–7:00.

Yusupovsky Palace (where Rasputin was killed)
Moika 94
Closed weekdays.
Hours: Saturday and Sunday, noon–4:30.

Literary, Theatrical, and Musical Museums

Akhmatova Museum
In a rear wing of the Sheremetyev Palace on the Fontanka
Closed Monday and the last Wednesday of each month.
Hours: 10:30–6:30 (last entry at 5:30).

Circus Museum
Fontanka 3
Closed Sunday.
Hours: noon–5:00.

Dostoyevsky Apartment Museum
Kuznechny Pereulok 5/2
Closed Monday.
Hours: 10:00–5:30.

Literary Museum in the name of Pushkin
Naberezhnaya Makarova
Closed Monday and Tuesday.
Hours: 11:00–5:30.

M u s e u m s

Musical Instruments Museum
Isaakiyevskaya Ploshad' 5
Closed Monday and Tuesday.
Hours: noon–6:00.

Pushkin Museum
Moika 12
Closed Tuesdays and the last Friday of each month.
Hours: 10:30–5:30 (last entry 4:30).
English language tours.

Rimsky-Korsakov Apartment Museum
Zagorodny Prospect 28, kv. 39
Closed Monday and Tuesday.
Hours: noon–6:00 (in summers closes at 5:00).

Russian Opera Museum (Fyodor Shaliapin Apartment)
Ulitsa Graftio 2b
Closed Monday and Tuesday.
Hours: 11:00–5:00.

Theatrical Museum
Ploshad' Ostrovskogo 6
Closed Tuesday.
Hours: noon–6:00.

Scientific Museums

Arctic and Antarctic Museum
Ulitsa Marata 24a
Closed Monday and Tuesday.
Hours: 10:00–5:00.

Anthropology and Ethnography Museum (Kunstkamera)
Universitetskaya Naberezhnaya 3

Closed Saturday and Sunday.
Hours: 11:00–5:00.

Botanic Garden of the Academy of Sciences
Ulitsa Professora Popova 2
Closed Friday.
Hours: 11:00–4:00 (in summers until 5:00).

Ethnography of the USSR Museum
Inzhinirnaya Ulitsa 4/1
Closed Monday.
Hours: Thursday 11:00–6:00, Friday 11:00–4:00; other days 11:00–5:00.

Zoological Museum
Universitetskaya Naberezhnaya 1
Closed Monday.
Hours: Tuesday 11:00–5:00; other days 11:00–6:00.

Estate and Palace Museums Outside the City (ideal for picnics):

Peterhof Palace and Park
In the town of Petrodvorets
Closed Monday.
Hours: 11:00–6:00.
One of the most spectacular palace-garden-fountain ensembles in the world. Be sure to get there early to ensure tickets to the main palace and many pavilions. It is possible to reach Petrodvorets by train from the Pribaltiyskaya Station, but the best way in ice-free months is by boat, from the dock directly in front of the Winter Palace.

Pushkin

The town of Pushkin (formerly Tsarkoye Selo) served as a summer resort for the czars. Russia's great poet got his schooling at an elite academy on the grounds. You can catch a train to the town in the Vitebsk Railway Station. Again, if you are not part of a tour group, get there early before the tickets run out. In the town you will find:

Catherine Palace
Closed Tuesday and the last Monday of each month.
Hours: 10:00–6:00.

Pushkin Museum and Lycée
Closed Thursday and the last Friday of each month.
Hours: 11:00–6:00.

Pushkin Dacha
Closed Tuesday.
Hours: 11:00–5:00.

Alexander Palace
Not open to the public.

Pavlovsk

Two miles from Pushkin, this palace-garden complex was built by Catherine the Great, particularly with the help of Scottish architect Charles Cameron. You can get there from the Vitebsk Station or by taking bus #280 from Pushkin Park to Pavlovsk Station. Try reading Suzanne Massey's *Pavlovsk* if you plan a trip. Be sure to reserve time for a walk around the grounds.

Grand Palace
Closed Friday and the first Monday of each month.
Hours: 10:30–5:00.

Lomonosov

Lomonosov is six miles from Petrodvorets, and is reached from the Pribaltiyskaya Railway station. Get off at the Oranienbaum stop. Catherine the Great's Chinese Palace alone is worth the trip. All the Lomonosov museums are closed Tuesdays and the last Monday of each month, with hours of 11:00–6:00. The Chinese Palace and the Coasting Hill Pavilion are closed October 15–May 15.

The Palace of Peter III, where the Emperor was when Catherine the Great mounted her coup against him, is open year-round. Alexander Menshikov's palace is closed to the public.

Theaters, Concert Halls, and Opera Houses

Except for the Bolshoi and the Kirov, tickets are often available right at the box office. With a few words of Russian, you can often acquire them. If you have trouble, ask the service bureau in your hotel or visit the main Intourist office in either Moscow or Leningrad to order tickets.

Moscow

Bolshoi
Teatralnaya (formerly Sverdlova) Ploshad' 2
Tel. 292-0050

Chamber Music Theater
Leningradsky Prospect 71
Tel. 198-7204

Children's Musical Theater
Prospect Vernadskogo 5
Tel. 930-5177

Children's Puppet Theater
Sadovaya Samotechnaya 3
Tel. 299-5373

Durov Animal Theater
Ulitsa Durova 4
Tel. 971-3047

Gypsy Theater
Leningradsky Prospect 32/2
Tel. 250-7334, 250-7353

Maly Theater
Teatralnaya (formerly Sverdlova) Ploshad' 1/6
Tel. 923-2621

Mayakovsky Theater
Ulitsa Gertsena 19
Tel. 290-6241

Moscow Arts Theater (MKhAT)
Khudozhestvennogo Teatralnogo Passazha 3
Tel. 229-8760

Moscow Circus (New)
Prospect Vernadskogo 17
Tel. 130-9676

Moscow Circus (Old)
Tsvetnoi Bulvar 13
Tel. 221-5880

Moscow Conservatory
Ulitsa Gertsena 13
Tel. 299-8183

Operetta Theater
Pushkinskaya Ulitsa 6
Tel. 229-9675

Theaters

Stanislavsky Musical Theater
Pushkinskaya Ulitsa 17
Tel. 229-4250

Tchaikovsky Concert Hall
Boshaya Sadovaya Ulitsa 20
Tel. 299-0378

Vakhtangov Theater
Arbat 26
Tel. 241-0728

Leningrad

Kirov Theater of Opera and Ballet
Teatralnaya Ploshad' 1
Tel. 216-5264

Bolshoi Dramatic Theater
Fontanka 65
Tel. 310-9242

Bolshoi Puppet Theater
Ulitsa Nekrasova 10
Tel. 273-6672

Kommisarzhevsky Theater
Ulitsa Rakova 19
Tel. 311-3102

Maly Dramatic Theater
Ulitsa Rubensteina 18
Tel. 314-3387

Maly Theater of Opera and Ballet
Ploshad' Iskusstva 1
Tel. 312-2040

Musical Comedy Theater
Ulitsa Rakova 13
Tel. 210-3680

Puppet Theater
Nevsky Prospect 52
Tel. 319-1900

Pushkin Theater of Drama (formerly Alexandrinsky)
Ploshad' Ostrovskogo
Tel. 312-1545

Theater of Comedy
Nevsky Prospect 56
Tel. 312-4555

Useful Words
and Phrases

(Spelled phonetically)

Yes	*DAH*
No	*NYET*
Good Morning	*DOH-bree-yeh OO-trah*
Good Day	*DOH-bree Dyen*
Good Evening	*DOH-bree VYEH-cher*
Goodbye	*dah Svee-DAHN-yeh*
Thank you	*Spah-SEE-bah*
Please	*Pah-ZHAL-ees-tah*
What?	*SHTOH?*
Street	*OO-leet-sah*
House	*DOHM*
Hotel	*Gahs-TEEN-ee-tsah*
Airport	*Ah-ehr-oh-PORT*
I am an American (man).	*YAH Ah-myer-yeh-KAHN-yets*
I am an American (woman).	*YAH Ah-myer-yeh-KAHN-kah*
Taxi	*Tak-SEE*

Useful Words and Phrases

I need a taxi.	Mnyeh NAH-dah tak-SEE.
Policeman	Mee-lee-tsee-oh-NYER
I need a policeman.	Mnyeh NOO-zhen mee-lee-tsee-oh-NYER.
I am ill.	YAH bahl-YEH-yu.
Hospital	GOHS-pee-tahl
I need an ambulance.	Mnyeh NOO-zhnah SKOH-rah-yah POH-mohsh
How much does it cost?	SKOHL-kah EH-tah STOH-eet?
My name is _____.	Men-YAH zah-VOOT _____.
Mr. _____	Gahs-pah-DEEN _____
Mrs. _____	Gahs-pah-ZHAH _____
Comrade _____	Toh-VAHR-eesh _____
Madame _____	Mah-DAHM _____
I love you.	YAH Teb-YAH Lyu-BLYU.
Where?	G-DYEH?
Where is the church?	G-DYEH TSER-kov?
Where is the museum?	G-DYEH Moo-ZYEH?
Where is the Kremlin?	G-DYEH KRYEH-mel?
Where is the metro?	G-DYEH Myeh-TROH?
Where is a telephone?	G-DYEH teh-leh-FOHN?
Excuse me.	Prah-STEE-tyeh.
What time is it?	Kah-TOR-ee chas?
Waiter	Ah-FEETS-ee-yant
Menu	MEN-yu
Wine	VEE-noh
Beer	PEE-vah
Vodka	VOHD-kah
Check	SHCHYOT
Restaurant	Res-toh-RAHN
Money	DYEHN-gee
Rubles	Roo-BLYEH
Dollars	DOH-lahr-ee
One	Ah-DEEN
Two	DVAH
Three	TREE
Four	Che-TEER-ee

Useful Words and Phrases

Five	*PYAT*
Six	*SHYEST*
Seven	*SYEM*
Eight	*VOH-Syem*
Nine	*DYEH-vyat*
Ten	*DYEH-syat*
Hundred	*STOH*
Thousand	*TEE-sach*

Sources

Moscow Walks

Walk 1—The Kremlin: A Tour of Its Ancient Buildings

Page 38: Archeological excavations on the Kremlin grounds are described in *Pamyatniki Arkhitekturi Moskvi: Kreml, Kitai-Gorod, Tsentralniye Ploshadi* (Moscow: Izdatelstvo Iskusstov, 1982), 21–27. About the reference to the wooden house without a chimney: 24. A map of archeological deposits in the Moscow region, including Arab money: 22.

Page 39: George Vernadsky asserts that Sophia Paleologue "proved very useful to Ivan in his dealings with Italian architects and technicians," *Russia at the Dawn of the Modern Age* (New Haven and London: Yale University Press, 1969), 26. Her sponsorship by the Pope and marriage to Ivan III: 19–21.

Sources

Page 41: Vernadsky describes Muscovy's subjugation of Novgorod: Vernadsky, 35–66.

Page 41: "The old and infirm men . . ." from *Notes Upon Russia by Sigismund Von Herberstein, Ambassador from the Court of Germany to the Grand Prince Vasily Ivanovich, In the years 1517 and 1526,* translated and edited by R. H. Major (London: Hakluyt Society, 1851–52), Book II, 65.

Page 44: The buildings and layout of Cathedral Square are described as a precedent for other cities in M. Iliyn, *Moscow: Monuments of Architecture of the 14th–17th Centuries* (Moscow: Izdatelstvo Iskusstvo, 1973), 30.

Page 51: "His upper garment . . .": Master Anthony Jenkinson's 1557 Record of a Voyage to Muscovy in *Principal Navigations Voyages and Discoveries of the English Nation* (London: Hakluyt Society, 1566), 337.

Page 51: Nikodim Kondakov describes the plight of painters commissioned to work in the Kremlin in *The Russian Icon* (Oxford: The Clarendon Press, 1927), 140–42.

Page 52: Although much confusion still remains, the symbolism and political significance of the frescoes in the Cathedral of the Annunciation is addressed in many sources, including: Vernadsky, *The Tsardom of Moscow 1547–1682* (New Haven and London: Yale University Press, 1969), 74–80; Benson Bobrick, *Fearful Majesty: The Life and Reign of Ivan the Terrible* (New York: Putnam), 1987, 132–37; and I. A. Zhuravleva, *Cathedral of the Annunciation* (Moscow: Vneshtorgizdat, 1989), 2 of English text. "You started with a crusade . . .": Vernadsky, *The Tsardom of Moscow,* 76.

Page 61: Kondakov, *The Russian Icon,* 143.

Walk 2—Red Square and Kitai Gorod

Page 69: The account of Stenka Razin's execution was written by Jacob Reitenfels, nephew of the Czar's doctor, as quoted by Laurence Kelly in *Moscow: A Travellers' Companion* (London: Constable, 1983), 159.

Page 71: "If you are just and pious . . .": *The Correspondence Between Prince Kurbsky and Tsar Ivan IV of Russia 1564–1579*, translated and edited by Fennell (Cambridge University Press, 1955), 19.

Page 72: Hagiographic stories: G. P. Fedotov, *Svyatiye Drevnei Rusi X-XVII Ct.* (New York: Izdaniye Russkogo Pravoslavnogo Bogoslovskogo Fonda, 1951), 199–202.

Page 74: "From early morning . . .": *Noviy Putovoditel po Moskve* (Moscow: V Universitetskoi Typographia, 1833), 160–61.

Page 75: "Our men beganne to wonder . . .": "The Voyages and Discoveries of Richard Chanceler," *Principal Navigations*, 286.

Page 76: The surveillance foreigners endured while in Moscow; in particular the watchmen's habit of burning fires to illuminate foreign residences: Bobrick, 56.

Page 79: For a discussion of Nikon's 1655 edict: Vernadsky, 765.

Page 80: The influence of civil architecture on seventeenth century churches is stressed by Iliyn, 39.

Pages 83–85: Descriptions of Shchukin and Ryabushinsky; the suicides of Savva Morozov and Shchukin relatives; execution of Tretyakov for espionage: Beverly Kean, *All the Empty Palaces* (London: Barrie and Jenkins, 1983), 148–51.

Sources

Page 87: The tribulations of setting up a printing press in Russia, Vernadsky, 77–78, 424–26.

Walk 3—Novodyevichi Convent

Page 100: "a deformed body . . .": Henri Troyat, *Peter the Great* (New York: Dutton, 1987), 11.

Page 103: The torture and execution of Captain Stepan Glebov, Evdokia's lover: Troyat, 228.

Page 109: Peter's repression following *streltsy* revolt and his dangling of corpses outside of Sophia's window: Troyat, 114–17.

Walk 4—From the Arbat to Kachalova Street

Page 121: "O tyrants of the world . . .": Ernest J. Simmons, *Pushkin* (New York: Vintage, 1964), 94; "not in the position of a prisoner": Simmons, 248; "What would you have done . . ." Simmons, 253; "She was tall . . .": Simmons, 338. The account of Pushkin is based on Simmons's biography.

Page 124: Melnikov's building techniques and expressionistic symbolism: S. Frederick Starr, *Melnikov: Solo Architect in a Mass Society* (Princeton: Princeton University Press, 1978), 117–27, 240–258.

Page 126: Description of the gendarme posts and the policemen: M. V. Davidov, "Moskva. Pyatdesyatiye i Shestdesyatiye Godi XIX Stoletiye," *Moskovskaya Starina* (Moscow: Izdatelstvo Pravda, 1989), 28–30.

Page 130: Passage from Lermontov's "Death of a Poet": Simmons, 437.

Page 133: Significance of the street names as marking settlements of Kremlin service workers is described under individual street listings by P. V. Sytin, *Iz Istorii Moskovskikh Ulits* (Moscow: Moskovskiy Rabochiy, 1958) and G. K. Efremov et al., *Imena Moskovskikh Ulits* (Moscow: Moskovskiy Rabochiy, 1988).

Page 135: Rumor that Gorky was killed by poisoned candy: Henri Troyat, *Gorky* (New York: Crown, 1989), 196–97.

Page 136: "These apprentices of fashion . . .": Marquis de Custine, *Empire of the Czar*, with introduction by George Kennan (New York: Doubleday, 1989), 311. Reprint of 1843 English translation of French original, *La Russie en 1839.*

Leningrad Walks

Walk 5—From the Pushkin Theater to the Square of the Arts

Page 150: Peter's decision to send students abroad for architectural training: James Cracraft, *The Petrine Revolution in Russian Architecture* (Chicago: University of Chicago Press, 1988), 161–62.

Page 151: Count Alexei Razumovsky's emergence from the chorus to become Elizabeth's lover, and his beatings of other nobles: M. I. Pilaev, *Stariy Peterburg* (St. Petersburg: Typographia Suvorina, 1889; facsimile reprint: Moscow: IKPA, 1990), 144–45. Elizabeth's domestic habits including her late hours and the ban on noisy traffic: 78. Catherine the Great gives the Anichkov Palace to Potemkin: 145.

Page 152: Robbers on the far side of the Fontanka: Pilaev, 154. Prince Beloselsky-Belozersky's work as a translator: 248.

Page 156: "I make no claim . . .": Anna Akhmatova, *Sochineniye V Dvukh Tomakh* (Moscow: Khudozhestvennaya Literatura, 1986), Book 1, 333 (translation by the authors).

Page 158: Razumovsky beat Count Shuvalov: Pilaev, 144.

Page 159: Quarrel between Lomonosov and Sumarokov, as quoted from Shuvalov memoirs: Pilaev 170–72.

Page 161: Description of the Mikhailovsky Palace: Custine, 180–81.

Walk 6 — From Kazan Cathedral to the Summer Palace

Page 168: Paul's insistence that Bernini's colonnade be incorporated; his initial choice of another architect (the Scott, Charles Cameron, designer of Pavlovsk); and switch to Voronikhin: P. Ya. Kann, *Kazanskaya Ploshad'* (Leningrad: Lenizdat, 1988), 28–30. Kann suggests that the switch may have been because of Paul's hatred for his mother, and by extension, one of her favorite architects: 33. Close ties between Stroganov and his serf, Voronikhin, whom he frees in 1786, and the insulting nickname: 31–32. Suggestion that Voronikhin was Stroganov's illegitimate son: Dmitri Sarabianov, *Russian Art from Neoclassicism to the Avant-Garde: 1800–1917* (New York: Harry Abrams, 1990), 12.

Page 169: Story about the weeping icon and Peter's reaction: Kann, 13–14. According to Kann, the Virgin of Kazan was at that point housed in the Church of the Trinity in another part of the city.

Page 170: "It was always known in advance . . .": Osip Mandelstam, "The Noise of Time" in *The Prose of Osip Mandelstam,* translated by Clarence Brown, (Princeton: Princeton University Press, 1965), 76.

Page 179: Peter's requirement that all citizens own a boat: V. S. Shvartz, *Arkhitekturniy Ansambl' Marsova Polya* (Leningrad: Izdatelstvo Iskusstvo, 1989), 8.

Page 179: Rapid pace of construction, at night lit by torches and lanterns; soldier's dream at the gates of the Summer Garden; stripping of the St. Isaac's Cathedral facade: Pilaev 379. Paul's humiliation of the military including Suvorov quote: 358–88. Difficulties of heating the castle interior due to rapid building: Shvartz, 78.

Page 181: Lights out and restrictions on meals: Shvartz, 63. Assassination of Paul: W. Bruce Lincoln, *The Romanovs* (New York: Anchor Books, 1981), 376–81.

Page 182: Design of the Summer Garden attributed to Peter: G. R. Bolotova, *Letniy Sad* (Leningrad: Khudozhnik RSFSR, 1988), 7; O. N. Kuznetsova and B. F. Borzin, *Letniy Sad i Letniy Dvorets Petra I* (Leningrad: Lenizdat, 1988), 10–11. Moscow, the Baltic, Siberia, and foreign countries mentioned as sources for trees: 13. Exotic and tropical trees, bushes, and flowers are ordered by, or sent as gifts to, Peter: 16.

Sources

Page 183: "Classicism became . . .": L. S. Aleshina, *Leningrad i Okrestnosti* (Moscow: Izdatelstvo Iskusstvo, 1980), 15–16. Drainage system and build-up of land: Kuznetsova and Borzin, 13.

Page 185: Paganism in the northern forests: Pilaev, 8. Summer Palace as a form of propaganda for Peter: Bolotova, 24.

Page 186: Allegorical meaning of Summer Palace bas reliefs: Kuznetsova and Borzin, 130–32.

Walk 7—Along the Left Bank of the Neva

Page 195: Nicholas interfered with technical and aesthetic questions: G. P. Butikov and G. A. Khvostova, *Isaakievskiy Sobor* (Leningrad: Lenizdat, 1974), 25–26. First wooden St. Isaac's Cathedral: 8. Stone St. Isaac's: 10.

Page 196: Rinaldi's St. Isaac's: Butikov and Khvostova, 12–13. "This monument to two reigns . . .": 14, as well as Pilaev, 380. (Translations by the authors.) Workers charge Nicholas during the Decembrists' Revolt, quoted from the Emperor's diary: Butikov and Khvostova, 65.

Page 202: "There is no liberal tradition finer . . .": George Kennan, "America and the Russian Future" (reprint of 1951 essay), *Foreign Affairs* (New York: Council on Foreign Relations, Spring 1990), 159.

Page 204: Dmitri Sarabianov discusses the symbolism of the Admiralty sculptures as well as the layout of the entire building: *Russian Art from Neoclassicism to the Avant-Garde, 1800–1917*, 14–15, 22–24.

Page 210: The mountain of trash and building materials given to the people, while Peter III watches: Pilaev, 175.

Page 213: Konstantin Stanislavsky, *My Life in Art,* translated by J. J. Robbins (New York: Little, Brown and Company, 1924), 12.

Page 215: "No illuminating statements . . .": Simmons, 431. "I love your severe, graceful appearance . . .": prose translation by Dmitri Obolensky, *The Heritage of Russian Verse* (Bloomington: Indiana University Press, 1976), 113. Reprint of 1965 Penguin edition.

Page 215: "The Czar, like any officer . . .": Simmons, 393.

Page 217: Circumstances of the duel and Pushkin's death: Simmons, 384–428; and D. S. Mirsky, *Pushkin* (New York: Dutton, 1963), 217–226.

INDEX

Index

Index

Index

Index

Index

THE HENRY HOLT WALKS SERIES

For people who want to *learn* when they travel, not just see.

Look for these other exciting volumes in Henry Holt's best-selling Walks series:

PARISWALKS, Revised Edition, by Alison and Sonia Landes
Five intimate walking tours through the most historic quarters of the City of Light.
288 pages, photos, maps $12.95 Paper

LONDONWALKS, Revised Edition, by Anton Powell
Five historic walks through old London, one brand new for this edition.
272 page, photos, maps $12.95 Paper

VENICEWALKS by Chas Carner and Alessandro Giannatasio
Four enchanting tours through one of the most perfect walking environments the world has to offer.
240 pages, photos, maps $12.95 Paper

ROMEWALKS by Anya M. Shetterly
Four walking tours through the most historically and culturally rich neighborhoods of Rome.
256 pages, photos, maps $12.95 Paper

FLORENCEWALKS by Anne Holler
Four intimate walks through this exquisite medieval city, exploring its world-famous art and architecture.
208 pages, photos, maps $12.95 Paper

VIENNAWALKS by J. Sydney Jones
Four walking tours that reveal the home of Beethoven, Freud, and the Habsburg monarchy.
304 pages, photos, maps $12.95 Paper